# Niccolò Machiavelli

## Twayne's World Authors Series

Carlo Golino, Editor

*University of Massachusetts*

TWAS 656

*Bust of Machiavelli by an unknown artist Florentine School, 16th century, formerly in the Accademia Colombaria, Florence.* Alinari photograph

# Niccolò Machiavelli

## By Silvia Ruffo-Fiore

*University of South Florida*

**Twayne Publishers • Boston**

*Niccolò Machiavelli*

Silvia Ruffo-Fiore

Copyright © 1982 by G. K. Hall & Company
Published by Twayne Publishers
A Division of G. K. Hall & Company
70 Lincoln Street
Boston, Massachusetts 02111

Book Production by Marne B. Sultz

Book Design by Barbara Anderson

**Library of Congress Cataloging in Publication Data**

Ruffo-Fiore, Silvia.
  Niccolò Machiavelli.

  (Twayne's world authors series ; TWAS 656)
  Bibliography: p. 166
  Includes index.
  1. Machiavelli, Niccolò, 1469–1527—Criticism and
interpretation.  I. Title.  II. Series.
PQ4627.M2Z79                858'.309                81–20256
ISBN 0–8057–6499–2                                    AACR2

*For Mafdi*

# Contents

# About the Author

Silvia Ruffo-Fiore is professor of English in the College of Arts and Letters, University of South Florida, Tampa, Florida. A native of Pittsburgh, Pennsylvania, she received the B.Ed. and M.A. from Duquesne University and the Ph.D. from the University of Pittsburgh. Her honors, awards, and grants include a Fulbright Study Grant, *Who's Who in America, Marquis Who's Who of Professional Women, Personalities of the South, Directory of American Scholars, Dictionary of International Biography,* a Folger Library Summer Grant, University of South Florida Research Council Award, selection by the 1976 University of South Florida Senior Class as one of the Ten Outstanding Professors, member of the Florida State Commission on the Status of Women. Her extensive professional involvement includes contributing editor of the *Pirandello Newsletter,* abstractor for the American Bibliographical Center–Clio Press, regional representative of the American Association of University Professors of Italian, reviewer for *Choice,* and membership in many professional organizations. She has published a major study, *Donne's Petrarchism: A Comparative View* (Florence: Grafica Toscana, 1976), many articles and reviews on Renaissance literature and women in literature, and has presented numerous scholarly papers here and abroad. She is presently compiling an annotated guide to modern criticism and scholarship on Machiavelli under the auspices of a grant from the National Endowment for the Humanities, Division of Research Programs.

# Preface

While recognizing the importance of Machiavelli's political and historical ideas, this book intends to make better known how the literary and rhetorical dimensions of his writings contribute to their meaning—how politics, history, and literature interacted. This critical overview surveys his writings, particularly stressing their literary qualities, in order to adjust popular, stereotyped views and to make his works more clearly understood and appreciated. Since much information exists on the background of this period, on the Medici, the Borgias, the Papacy, and other significant people and happenings that affected Machiavelli's work, the main events of his life and times are discussed only in terms of how they molded his purpose and thought and how they illuminate his meaning and style. This study interprets and assesses the major and some of the minor works, using his official writings, such as the *Legations,* and his official and personal letters, to supplement, support, and exemplify certain premises. Four principles have guided the screening and selection of materials to be included in this overview: (1) to show the meaningful and unifying interrelationships in the entire Machiavelli canon; (2) to present his works within an informing historical, political, and literary context, while also suggesting reasons for their perennial appeal; (3) to modify oversimplified or misconceived views which neglect the interdependence of ideology and art in Machiavelli's writings; (4) to indicate the extraordinary range of his historical impact. The book is designed to inform unfamiliar readers and to redirect already acquainted ones. While acknowledging valuable traditional perspectives which continue to enrich an understanding of Machiavelli's work, this examination also offers approaches qualifying, expanding, and even rejecting conventional views, and suggests areas for further investigation.

I would like to express my admiration, respect, and thanks to all Machiavelli scholars, many cited here, for their stimulating, inspiring studies, without which this brief treatment would not have been possible. My thanks extend to the following who have contributed to the writing of this book: the University of South Florida Research Council and English Department for funds and for time off from teaching to do research; the Folger Library for a Summer Fellowship; the Interlibrary Loan Staff of my university library, particularly James Vastine and Florence Jandreau for their invaluable assistance in accumulating materials; my editor, Carlo L. Golino, for his patient, meticulous review of the manuscript; and Elizabeth Melton, my remarkable assistant, for her cheerful willingness and keenly observant eye. My deepest gratitude goes to my dearest friend, who also happens to be my husband, Mafdi, for his unremitting encouragement, sensitive perception, extensive knowledge, unselfish love, and "Machiavellian wit."

Silvia Ruffo-Fiore

*University of South Florida*

# Chronology

| 1469 | Birth in Florence. |
|------|---------------------|
| 1498 | Hears Savonarola's lent sermons and writes to Ricciardo Becchi. Elected Chancellor of the Second Chancellery and Chancellor and Secretary of the Ten of Liberty and Peace. |
| 1499 | Legation to Jacopo d'Appiano, Florentine mercenary. *Discourse to the Ten on Pisan Affairs.* Legation to Caterina Sforza. |
| 1500 | First Legation to France. |
| 1501–1502 | Mission to Pistoia and *Report on the Pistoia Factions.* Mission to Siena. Marries Marietta di Ludovico Corsini. |
| 1502 | Missions to Cesare Borgia. Piero Soderini made *Gonfaloniere* of Florence. |
| 1503 | Continues Legation to Cesare Borgia. Usual date assigned to *Discourse on the Rebellious Peoples of Valdichiana* and to *Description of the Method Used by Duke Valentino in Killing Vitellozzo Vitelli, Oliverotto da Fermo,* etc. *Words to Be Spoken on the Law for Appropriating Money.* First Legation to Rome. |
| 1504 | Second Legation to France. *The First Decade.* |
| 1505 | Missions to Baglione, Gonzaga, and Petrucci. Sent to the Siege of Pisa. |
| 1506 | Attempts to organize a Florentine militia. *Discourse on How to Arm the State of Florence. Discourse on the Ordinance and on the Florentine Militia.* Second Legation to Rome ( Julius II). |
| 1507 | Made Chancellor of the Nine in charge of the militia. First Legation to Maximilian. |

| | |
|---|---|
| 1508 | *Report on Germany.* Continues organization of militia. |
| 1509 | Pisa surrenders to Florence. Second Legation to Maximilian. Possible date for *The Second Decade. Discourse on Germany and the Emperor.* |
| 1510 | Third Legation to France. *Report on French Affairs* and *On the Nature of the French* (?). |
| 1511 | Fourth Legation to France. |
| 1512 | *Report on German Affairs.* Sack of Prato, fall of Florence and Soderini, return of Medici. Dismissed from offices. |
| 1513 | Boscoli-Capponi anti-Medicean plot. Arrest, imprisonment, torture, release. Retires to San Casciano. Begins the *Discourses. The Prince.* |
| 1514–1516 | *Discourse on the Language.* |
| 1517–1518 | *The Golden Ass.* Completes *Discourses on Livy.* |
| 1518 | Frequents Orti Oricellari. *Mandragola.* Possibly begins *The Art of War.* |
| 1519 | *Discourse on Reforming the Government of Florence.* |
| 1520 | *Belfagor. Summary of Lucchesi Affairs. Life of Castruccio Castracani.* Receives commission from Giulio de' Medici to write the history of Florence. Possibly completes *The Art of War.* |
| 1521 | Publication of *The Art of War.* |
| 1523 | Publication of Agostino Nifo's plagiary of *The Prince, De regnandi peritia.* Meets Barbara Raffacani Salutati. |
| 1525 | *Clizia* performed in Florence. Presents *History of Florence* to Clement VII. |
| 1526 | Appointed Secretary of the Five of the Walls. *Report on the Fortifications of Florence.* |
| 1527 | Death in Florence and burial in Santa Croce. |

# Chapter One
# Machiavelli's Early Political Experiences and Writings

## Machiavelli's Youth: 1469–1497

The Machiavelli family originated in the town of Montespertoli near Val di Pesa south of Florence.[1] The branch of the family from which Niccolò Machiavelli descended originated with Dono Machiavelli. The family came into property by a bequest in 1393 by Ciango dei Castellani of Montespertoli (another branch of the family) to Buoninsegna and Lorenzo, children of Filippo Machiavelli, Niccolò Machiavelli's great-great-grandfather. Although the inheritance carried privileges and rights of patronage, it was of little value particularly when divided among the family branches. Bernardo Machiavelli, Niccolò's father, inherited lands in San Casciano outside Florence along with some houses in the city, among them one on Via Guicciardini, number 16 near Ponte Vecchio, where Niccolò intermittently lived and later died.

The family had a history of political and civic involvement, contributing over the years twelve *gonfalonieri* ("burgess") and fifty-four priors. Although the family was not nobility, they were considered *popolani grassi*, rich commoners, and possessed a coat of arms from which their name derived. The arms bore a blue cross in a silver field, with four blue nails at the four corners of the cross (*mal chiavelli, malclavelli, malchiavelli*, various versions of the Italian for "bad nails,"[2] probably referring to the cruel nails pounded into Christ's body on the cross).

Bernardo Machiavelli, Niccolò's father, born in 1428, was a tax lawyer and served as Treasurer of the Marches. After inheriting the property from his uncle Totto, son of Buoninsegna Machiavelli, in

1458 Bernardo married Bartolomea, widow of Niccolò Bennizzi,
and daughter of Stefano dei Nelli. Bernardo was a thrifty man, if
not miserly. His *Libro di Ricordi*,[3] which records his family and
business memoirs from September 30, 1471, to August 19, 1487,
paints him as a meticulous, somewhat cultured man, preoccupied
about money and his children's education. Bernardo and Bartolomea
had four children, two daughters, Primavera and Margherita, respectively five years and two years older than Niccolò, and another
son, Totto, six years younger than Niccolò. Although the family
could not afford luxuries, Bernardo's interest in studies led him to
buy books in the cheaper loose form and then have them bound and
sometimes even illuminated. Bartolomea, likewise, had some education, for she wrote poetry mostly on religious subjects, some of
which she dedicated to her son Niccolò.

Niccolò was born on May 3, 1469, in the same year that Piero
de' Medici, Cosimo's son, died. Little is known of Niccolò's child-
hood except what is recorded in Bernardo's *Libro*. On May 6, 1476,
the *Libro* records that Niccolò, then seven, began his study of the
"*Donatello*," the standard textbook for Latin. In the following year
he learned grammar and in January 1479 took up arithmetic.[4] It
is unlikely that Niccolò ever learned Greek, but he developed a great
interest in the reading of histories and at twelve, when he was writing
Latin compositions, Bernardo borrowed a copy of Justin, the first
history book children read. In determining the nature and scope of
Niccolò's early education, it is noteworthy that Bernardo bought
or owned copies of Livy, Macrobius, Priscian, Donato Acciaioli on
the *Ethics* of Aristotle, the *Deche* of Biondo; he borrowed the *Philippics,
De officiis, De oratore,* the *Ethics* of Aristotle, the *Cosmography* of
Ptolemy, a *Pliny* in translation, Justin, Biondo's *Italia Illustrata,*
and strangely enough, the Bible.[5] In his *Libro* Bernardo records how
in late June 1486 he sent Niccolò, then seventeen years old, to the
binders with a copy of the first three *Decades* of Livy's history of
Rome,[6] from which some twenty years later Niccolò would draw
in the writing of his *Discourses*. From what is known of the books
in the Machiavelli household, of the curriculum Renaissance young
men studied, and of the references found in Machiavelli's later writings, he probably read Livy, Caesar, Cicero, Tacitus, Suetonius,

Virgil, Ovid, Tibullus, and Catullus, and the Latin translations of
Polybius, Herodotus, Plutarch, Thucydides, Diogenes, Laertius,
Curtius Rufus, Xenophon, Aristotle, Sallust, and Horace.[7]

Practically nothing is known of Niccolò's life after this period
until 1497, just before he entered public service, with the exception
that on October 11, 1496, his mother died. It has been recently
shown that he may have spent most of the years from 1487 to 1495
in Rome, in the service of a Florentine banker, Berto Berti.[8] Beginning as an apprentice and promoted to cashier in 1493, Niccolò
revealed a potential for business; however, Berti's death in 1495
ended his employment with legal proceedings to gain monies owed
to him. In 1498 Niccolò returned to Florence never again to work
in the business world.

The historical and political developments of the fifteenth and
early sixteenth centuries, especially those in Florence, significantly
influenced Machiavelli's life and writings. The increasing spiritual
and civic corruption coupled paradoxically with a splendid cultural
rebirth in Florentine life provided him with the testimony of recent
times on which he would partially base the conclusions of his mature
writings. Florence had a long history of republicanism, and although
at times the people heeded more its nominal rituals, generally the
ruling nobles respected republican institutions. Florence became the
seat of the new humanism, a renewed love for liberty, individual
identity combined with civic virtue, and a rebirth of appreciation
for antiquity.

The Medici, particularly Lorenzo Il Magnifico, were greatly responsible for the fruition of Florence's commercial, artistic, and
political resources. The Medici descendants, especially Piero II, however, lacked the restraint, tact, and discipline of the older generation,
and with each succeeding heir the deficiencies became more evident.
During the first fifty years of their rule they succeeded by scrupu-
lously observing the city's entrenched social and political traditions.
By preserving the appearance of democracy, carefully avoiding suspicion, jealousy, and envy, manipulating government institutions,
entering expedient marriages, and cultivating the favor of supporters, the family ruled by consensus rather than by force. These favored
followers contributed to the Medici defeat of the Neroni and Pazzi

conspiracies. They pursued a policy of peace, using mercenaries only when necessary, avoiding the expense and dangers of a standing army, and channelling these monies into the arts. This military practice would, however, weaken Florence later, yet at their peak they adroitly mingled politics, commerce, arts, and civics.

Factions, hereditary rule, economic weakening, and foreign intervention conspired to bring Florence to disaster. Internal dissension became an unstabling force with Piero II, who unwisely neglected the powerful, proud Florentine families who had traditionally shared in the government. The quasi-utopian conditions during the time of Cosimo and Lorenzo may also have contributed to a weakening of the people's moral and spiritual fiber. Lorenzo catered to lethargy and self-indulgence by sponsoring splendid festivals, games, and tournaments. Moreover, Florence's commitment to commerce and profit contributed to moral corruption. The profit, for which Florentine merchants greedily rivaled with their Italian counterparts, prevented peninsular unity, undermined Florentine political and social institutions, and weakened its foreign bargaining and trading position. The Papacy offered little positive modeling, while Medici political usurpation had allowed the citizens few opportunities to practice their republican institutions. The extravagance, opulence, and gaiety of the Medici court camouflaged both the potential for political chaos and the grim reality of disease, poverty, and death.[9] Florentine republicanism and humanism together with Medicean politics operated as formative aspects in Machiavelli's writings. Upon this scene of growing degeneracy in Italy and Florence the prophetic, terrifying voice of Savonarola was raised.

## Machiavelli Hears the Voice of Savonarola

Savonarola arrived in Florence from Ferrara in 1482 and lived in the city without arousing controversy until 1487, when Medici extravagances and Roman corruption became more blatant. In 1492 he began to preach against tyranny, injustice, and vices in Florence and Rome. Lorenzo de' Medici's failing health was of more concern than silencing the Friar. Whether Savonarola denied absolution to the dying Lorenzo remains speculation, but he did prophesize the invasion of Italy and with the coming of Charles VIII in 1494 the ominous prophecy was fulfilled. Charles, imagining himself a second Charlemagne, initiated his crusade ostensibly to reestablish the empire under French rule. His grandiose dreams were nurtured in Milan by Lodovico Sforza whose self-glorifying ambitions had been contained as long as Lorenzo, the "balancing needle," lived. This is the main point of Machiavelli's final comment in *The History of Florence* on the evils of Lodovico's ambition and the devastation which followed Lorenzo's death. [10]

Savonarola's role in the coming of Charles was more than that of prophet, since it was through his efforts as ambassador to the French king that Charles once in Florence did not activate his threat to sack the city and become its master. [11] Despite opposition by those in authority, the Friar's well-attended pulpit sermons [12] inspired a series of internal reforms leading to the formation of a republican constitution and government. [13] His visionary sermons and bitter denunciations of luxury, greed, and tyranny fostered internal dissension and inspired the wrath of Rome, whom he had condemned for its corruption and simony. Finally, in May 1497, the Friar was excommunicated [14] and forbidden to preach for advocating heresy. Coincidentally, on the same day as the excommunication, word reached Florence of the murder of Pope Alexander VI's son, the Duke of Gandia, news viewed by the superstitious and fanatical supporters of Savonarola as a sure sign of the Pope's error. [15]

During his period of forced silence his influence declined, while his enemies, known as the *arrabbiati,* grew stronger. His flair for accurate prophecy, his eloquence and self-confidence, his appeal both to the religious impulses of sensation seekers and the Florentine desires for liberty, prestige, and status, especially after the Charles affair, explained his previous ascendancy. These reasons coupled with his criticism of the Medici, which ingratiated those families whom the Medici had excluded from the government, and persistent condemnation of Alexander's papacy along with his call for self-abnegation and spiritual regeneration had consolidated a substantial group of Florentines called *piagnoni* ("wailers" or "snivelers") or *frateschi.* The papal sanctions, Medici supporters, and other brewing opposition eventually proved too much, however. Many condemned the hysterical events of February 7, 1497, when at his exhortations the "Burning of the Vanities" occurred in Piazza della Signoria during which rare books, manuscripts, paintings, sculptures, etc., were senselessly destroyed.

In early March 1498, after he was once again allowed to preach, Savonarola delivered two Lent sermons in San Marco attended by Machiavelli, whose evaluation is preserved in a letter, his first public writing treating political issues, to his friend Ricciardo Becchi, ambassador to the papal court. The sermons were the friar's final, desperate attempt to regain power. A month later on April 7, 1498, Savonarola was forced to accept the challenge of a rival brother of the Franciscan order at Santa Croce to live up to the claim that to prove the truth of his words he would walk through fire unscathed. Preparations were made in the Piazza della Signoria for this phenomenal event—the Trial by Fire—attended by many spectacle-seeking Florentines. A controversy arose, however, as to whether the Dominican friar and his colleagues should enter the flames holding the Host. No agreement could be reached and the vehemence of both groups was drowned by a sudden thunderstorm. The frustrated citizens became enraged, mobbed the streets, and attacked the friar's convent of San Marco.[16] Savonarola was arrested, interrogated, tortured, and tried, and on May 23, 1498, he was hanged and burned at the stake in the Piazza, the place now marked with a small commemorative plaque.

At the age of twenty-nine Machiavelli produced his first dated political document, an evaluation of two sermons in which he unmasks what he believed were the friar's contradictory and false statements. The first sermon, replete with emotional and fanatical appeals, was designed to unify his supporters against the newly elected Signoria which the friar anticipated would side with the Papacy against him.[17] Once the Signoria wrote to the Pope in support of Savonarola, in the second sermon he expediently rallied the Florentines against the Pope.

In a detached but critical manner, Machiavelli anatomizes Savonarola's themes and rhetorical strategems. He cites the friar's manipulation of biblical exegesis in referring to the words from Exodus ("The more they afflicted them, the more they multiplied and grew." I, 12) and to Moses' killing of an Egyptian (Exodus 2:

11–12). With terseness and irony he uncovers the friar's exploitation of the biblical text to authenticate his claims and to justify his actions. Machiavelli mingles his pungent analysis with what seems in some cases to be direct quotation of the friar's words, while in others he paraphrases,[18] thus exposing the dramatized religious emotionalism of the political appeal. Machiavelli's irony results from his literal adherence to Savonarola's text and oratorical style, heightening the friar's contradictions and demonstrating how they annihilate the religious content of the sermons.[19] The slightest detail does not escape Machiavelli's criticism as, for example, his penetrating comment on the friar's use of digression. Machiavelli's incisive analysis exposes how religion, threats based on superstition, and prophecy can be applied to a political end, especially when the people are susceptible to supernaturalism. Although later Machiavelli selectively endorses this technique, in this early letter, he is skeptical at the intrusion of religion into politics. It is important that at this incipient stage of his life and writings the subject should concern the relationship between religion and politics—so controversial in his later writings—and should mention Moses, the archetypal religious and political leader often mentioned in his later writings. On one level, Machiavelli, who would seem to prefer reason and logic over religicized politics, condemns Savonarola for his hypocrisy, cloak changing, and lies, while on another level, with a certain fascination admires his calculated use of religion.[20] This early work reveals significant traits which would characterize Machiavelli's later writings. He shows a tendency to view every situation in political terms, an aversion for emotionalism and invective as substitutes for reason, and an ironic tone in his analysis of religion and lies as political weapons.

The relationship between Savonarola and Machiavelli has been of consistent interest to critics down through the years.[21] Machiavelli could not have sympathized with the *piagnoni* or with Savonarola's conception of a theocratic tyranny, of a New Jerusalem with Christ at its head. Soon after Savonarola's death Machiavelli assumed his first government position, elected supposedly because of his neutrality in the Savonarola episode. Although he may have secretly revered the friar, Machiavelli believed that he had failed as a prophet and leader because he politicized his prophecies, while insufficiently arming them with military strength.

Machiavelli's letter to Becchi is interesting when viewed within the context of his later comments on Savonarola. Two years after his death Machiavelli composed the lines in the *Decennale* [The Decades] on Savonarola.[22] In a letter to Francesco Vettori on December 19, 1513, Machiavelli sardonically muses on the activities in Florence of a Franciscan preacher, Francesco da Montepulciano, whose sermons remind him of Savonarola's revivalist threats and prophecies.[23] On May 17, 1521, in writing to Guicciardini on his selection of a preacher for Florence, he again humorously implies a cynical evaluation of Savonarola.[24] In the *Discourses* Machiavelli analyzes the role of religion in establishing a strong state, in achieving, consolidating, and maintaining power. In discussing how a wise prince should provide against weak successors (I, 11), he is reminded of Savonarola's fate.[25] Machiavelli's most damning observation on Savonarola appears in I, 45, where he shows how he set a bad example by disobeying his own law of appeal in the 1497 episode regarding the five condemned Medicean plotters.[26] Machiavelli's final comment on Savonarola, III, 30, exposes the friar's lack of political experience, preparation, and awareness, and explains why Machiavelli saw him as a "unarmed prophet" who sought to rule with words alone. In this memorable discussion of how envy can impede a potentially beneficial leader from achieving success, Machiavelli links Savonarola first to Moses, a political and religious model both for him and the friar, and then to Soderini, the Florentine *gonfaloniere* who headed the state during much of Machiavelli's political life and whose failures caused Machiavelli's removal from office. Machiavelli believed these three men were faced with the same problem in their efforts to rule republics.[27] Since the friar's followers did not understand the political problem as he did, they failed to delegate to him the necessary power he lacked resulting from his priestly vocation.

These passages demonstrate that as a young man of twenty-nine Machiavelli had been impressed by Savonarola's rule and that later he scrutinized the reasons for his failure. Some claim that Machiavelli was familiar with Savonarola's *Treatise on the Government of Florence,* written in defense of the 1494 post-Medicean republic, and that Machiavelli owes many of the ideas in *The Prince* to this work.[28] Yet Machiavelli's earlier unfavorable evaluation of Savonarola in the Becchi letter altered later. The two men shared an apocalyptic world-view and an idealistic hope for renewal which Machiavelli reveals in *The Prince*, 26, where he employs the language of the prophetic millennialists such as Savonarola.[29] Machiavelli's later writings show that not only did he hear Savonarola's resounding words, but also that he learned much from them.

## Early Legations and Discourses

**Early Missions and the *Discourse on Pisa*.** Savonarola's death heralded the beginning of Machiavelli's life as a Florentine government official. But already in 1497 his abilities were recognized by his own family who entrusted him with the writing of a letter in behalf of the *Malclavellorum familia* to Giovanni Lopez, Cardinal of Perugia, to support their claims to the area of Pieve di Fagna, against the contested claims of the Pazzi family.[30] Although the letter betrays its writer's immaturity, it reveals the stylistic power for which Machiavelli would become distinguished. The letter succeeded and his family preserved its property rights. Following an unsuccessful attempt on February 19, 1498, as one of the candidates for First Secretaryship, Machiavelli, seemingly without a period of political apprenticeship, was formally elected to the post of Secretary to the Second Chancery on June 18, 1498, replacing Alessandro Braccesi.[31] Although the opponents were more experienced and Machiavelli was relatively unknown without a background in law or notaries as was the custom for this position, his political neutrality and his reputation as a man of letters may have contributed to his election.

While the First Chancery dealt with foreign affairs, the Second Chancery, to a certain extent dependent upon the First Chancery, handled internal affairs. Its officials were public servants rather than politically affiliated, charged with implementing policy made by others. The office of "secretary" was a flexible administrative position delegated with the formulation, the passing on and carrying through of orders. Although the duties entailed a substantial amount of office paper work, secretaries could and often were sent on missions abroad.

In light of the frequent governmental turnover in Florence, the secretaries provided a much needed continuity among the changing executives.[32] Machiavelli's duties were never really defined, varying according to need, and in July 1498 he assumed the added post of Secretary to the *Dieci di Balìa* ("The Ten of Power"), sometimes called the *Dieci di Libertà e di Pace,* a permanent government agency in charge of strategy, diplomacy, and war.[33] Machiavelli was paid 192 *fiorini di suggello,* equal to 128 gold florins; his salary increased slightly with the additional appointments, but throughout his career it remained too low for his responsibilities. His loyal assistant from the beginning was Biagio Buonaccorsi, a clerk, copyist, and reporter of the proceedings of the *Signoria.* The First Secretary or Chancellor of the Republic and highest ranking government official was Marcello Virgilio Adriani, several years older than Machiavelli, a learned teacher of classical studies who may have been Machiavelli's teacher at one time and who also may have suggested his name for election to office.[34]

Machiavelli's first foreign assignment was on March 24, 1499, when he was sent to settle a dispute with Jacopo d'Appiano, a *condottiero* (hired mercenary leader) of Florence. The next mission occurred on July 12 of the same year when he was sent to Forlì to speak with thrice widowed and tough-minded Caterina Sforza on the rehiring of her *condottiero* son, Ottaviano Riario.[35] The most important of Machiavelli's 1499 foreign assignments was to Pisa, from which resulted his *Discourse to the Ten on Pisan Affairs,* probably composed between April and June 1499. The history of Florence's conflict with Pisa was long and complex, the two cities having been enemies for some 300 years before Florence conquered Pisa in 1406; the situation was, however, aggravated by Charles VIII's agreement after his conquest of Naples in 1494 to protect Pisa against Florence. Charles hoped to force Florence to adhere to its alliance with him. Charles assigned to Pisa a French governor, d'Entragues, who sympathized with the Pisan desire for independence from Florence. Pisa had always been an important outlet for Florentine trade, especially at this time with shrinking markets and other Florentine territories seeking foreign assistance in their attempts at independence. The hostilities between the two cities reached a crucial point in January

1496, when d'Entragues returned the Pisan citadel to its citizens. War was the only alternative for Florence to win back Pisa.[36]

The *Discourse on Pisa* introduces what would later become Machiavelli's typical method of analyzing a political situation. He subdivides each question into two extreme and opposite hypotheses; the solution resulting from each is carefully considered while the intermediate cases or instances are ignored. By employing the "either-or" method he rejects middle-of-the-road compromises. The method conveys a tone of scientific rigor, of the objective search for a universal truth inherently present in the concrete, particular instance. The ideas of the *Discourse* derive from common military views, yet they are enlivened by the strength of Machiavelli's analytical powers and luminous style—qualities later to typify *The Prince* and the *Discourses*.[37] Machiavelli inductively draws from the specific historical event a determined, axiomatic lesson; within the situation he limits the axiom's scope by defining its extremes and its opposites; he negates compromise and the *via media* as methods of solution. The robust style—his presentation of the accrued political and military wisdom of the experience—is marked by an unclouded analytical vision, clear insights of motives and ends, and an incisive, sometimes ironical tone. His style, possibly the first example of modern prose, anticipates the good qualities of the so-called Senecan, or anti-Ciceronian style which characterizes the writing of Bacon and Montaigne. The significance of these early political experiences is found in (1) what they reveal about the sources of Machiavelli's later pronouncements on political and military questions, and (2) what they show about his stylistic development, and about the essential stylistic unity between his political and literary writings.[38]

**Borgia Legation and *A Description of the Method Used by Duke Valentino in Killing Vitellozzo Vitelli, Oliverotto Da Fermo, and Others.*** From the beginning Machiavelli's life seemed destined to be influenced by some of the most prominent historical figures of the age. Although he never met Lorenzo the Magnificent, the legend of his splendid rule, initiating in the same year as Machiavelli's birth and ending in 1492 when Machiavelli was twenty-three years old, permeated the politically volatile Florentine scene. As Machiavelli acknowledges in his *History of Florence,* Lorenzo had succeeded in achieving peaceful stability. He seemed like a wise mythic ruler from a remote past, like Theseus or Cyrus. The fiery, controversial Savonarola offered Machiavelli not only the opportunity to whet his political consciousness, but also the clear example of the well-intentioned leader who failed. The historical figure who more than any other would sharpen Machiavelli's ideas on effective political action was Cesare Borgia, the son of the Spanish Pope Alexander VI (Roderigo Borgia became Pope on August 11, 1492) and the Roman courtesan Vannozza Cattanei.

The chronicle of the Borgia family was shrouded in mystery and infamy. Rumors and scandals permeated the lives of Alexander's four children. Cesare had purportedly murdered his brother, Juan, the Duke of Gandia, whose brutally mutilated body was discovered in the Tiber River on June 14, 1497. Consistent with the Borgia reputation for nepotism, his father conferred the hat of cardinal on Cesare, but he renounced it and Holy Orders on August 13, 1498, to pursue a military and political life. It was also rumored that he had vyed with his brother and father for the favors of his sister, the equally infamous Lucrezia. Cesare was also supposedly responsible for the murder of Lucrezia's husband, the Duke of Bisceglie, on July 15, 1500.[39]

That year also marked the beginning of Cesare's expansionist campaigns to reconquer lost papal territories and to unite Italy under one rule. As a result of his capture of the seemingly invincible Caterina Sforza and of Faenza, the Pope made him Duke of Romagna. His haughty incursion into Tuscan territory in May 1500, following success against Bologna, forced the Florentines to call up troops from the surrounding countryside, unqualified to face Borgia's seasoned, organized soldiers. France's determination under Louis XII to reconquer Naples from the Spanish further complicated the Borgian threat to Florentine autonomy. By August 1501, France had succeeded and the Neapolitan ruler, Frederick, resigned his kingdom and retired to France. Borgia flaunted papal sanctioning of his military campaign and the backing of Florence's traditional, though at times unworthy ally, France. Florence's relations with France had been clouded by the city's refusal to pay 50,000 ducats which Louis XII would have used to defray the costs of the Naples campaigns.

In addition, Florence feared that Borgia's friendship with the exiled Piero de' Medici might precipitate an attack intended to impose Medicean tyranny.[40]

Machiavelli's private life during 1500–1501 also presented significant events: his father died in May 1500, and while on his French mission his sister married. Upon his return from France in August 1501, he married Marietta di Ludovico Corsini, a loyal, devoted wife and nurturing, affectionate mother to the six children she eventually bore. Bernardo, Baccia, Ludovico, Piero, and Guido survived and Baccia's son, Giuliano, preserved many of Machiavelli's writings. During 1501 his private life was periodically interrupted by missions in February, July, and October to Pistoia, where riots had erupted between leading rival families. As a result of his experiences there, Machiavelli would write a *Report on the Florentine Republic's Efforts to Suppress the Pistoia Factions* (1502). In August 1501, he was sent on his first legation to Siena to confer with Pandolfo Petrucci, one of Borgia's allies. The ominous shadow of Cesare Borgia in central Italy now threatened the Florentine Republic. In the spring of 1502 Borgia, assisted by Piero de' Medici and Vitellozzo Vitelli, the brother of Florence's victim during the Pisa episode, Paolo Vitelli, conquered Arezzo, on Florence's doorstep. Although Cesare renounced any part in the capture of Arezzo, claiming Vitelli had done it to avenge his brother's death, Borgia was not unhappy that the Florentines believed him responsible. Both Cesare and his father had consistently pressured Florence to dispatch ambassadors to both courts. Florence, with its strategic propinquity to Romagna, represented an important state with which to establish friendly relations in Cesare's efforts to reconquer papal territories and unify Italy. The Florentines acquiesced by sending Alessandro Bracci as ambassador to Rome, but there was much controversy, first as to the sagacity of sending an ambassador empowered to make agreements with Cesare whose terms might eventually prove disadvantageous or embarrassing, and second, as to whom to send. Machiavelli was dispatched as a special envoy to report the duke's actions and temporize the situation.

Machiavelli first met Borgia at Urbino, conquered by the duke in June 1502, when, with Cardinal Francesco Soderini, he spent two days in the Borgia camp. Even during this brief visit Machiavelli was impressed by the duke's quick, resolute manner. The first letter written during this initial Legation to Borgia and composed on June 22, 1502, before Machiavelli had formally met him, reflects impressions derived only from having heard about his political and military methods and success.[41] The classical and literary tone stresses the duke's qualities of celerity, subtlety, tenaciousness, and surprise. Near the end of the second letter—a lengthy account of the various conversations between the duke and the two envoys—Machiavelli praises Borgia's military and political *virtù*.[42] Borgia arrogantly demanded that Florence openly ally itself with him, pay him a large sum for his military services, and reinstate the Medici. After Machiavelli reported the duke's threats and demands, he returned to Florence while Soderini remained.

Machiavelli's brief encounter with Borgia heightened for him the strident contrast between the ineffectiveness of his own state and the intimidating, determined actions of the duke. The psychological, political, and military pressure of the Borgia crisis contributed to the surfacing of Florence's internal problems. To protect against the rise of another Piero de' Medici, the Constitution provided for a rotation system which brought new men into important offices every two months. This resulted in impermanence and inefficiency, fostered factional strife, aggravated the conflict between the rich and poor, undermined Florence's international image, and was counterproductive in developing experience and a sense of responsibility among those holding government positions. To curb the strife, suspicions, recriminations, and incompetence which had brought the city-Republic to veritable collapse, on August 26 a permanent *gonfaloniere* was instituted to guide governmental reform and reassure foreign powers. Of the main candidates for the position the most moderate, least controversial and offensive was selected on September 20, 1502, Piero Soderini, the brother of Machiavelli's colleague on the recent Borgia legation. Soderini had extensive government experience and although his family in the past had sided with the interests of the *ottimati,* the principal citizens and privileged rich, against the tyrannical ambitions of the Medici, Soderini proved more in favor of the popular, republican rule. The center majority which had selected him had undoubtedly considered that he had no party affiliations, no children and few relatives to claim hereditary rights. Yet his cautious, hesitant, and dilatory manner hampered his effectiveness. Soderini, who admired and liked Machiavelli, gradually, and perhaps unfortunately for the secretary, became more dependent on him. Eventually, Machiavelli would be known as Soderini's *mannerino*, thus irrevocably tying their fates. Although Machiavelli initially respected Soderini as Florence's much-needed permanent leader, as he came to know his weaknesses, Machiavelli's attitude grew more ambivalent. Soderini, with all his indecision and uncertainty, continued to hold this position until the 1512 reinstatement of the Medici.

While Florence was having constitutional and domestic problems, Borgia's military success was not without its own difficulties. His easy conquest of Urbino had aroused fear in his own *condottieri* as to their fate and that of the territories they claimed. In September 1502, as he prepared to attack Bologna, a conspiracy was formed by Orsini, Vitelli, Baglioni, Guidobaldo di Montefeltro of Urbino, Oliverotto da Fermo, Pandolfo Petrucci, and Giovanni Bentivoglio of Bologna. The conspirators seized the fortress of San Leo and held a meeting at Magione near Perugia on October 9 (a meeting later referred to by Borgia as the *dieta di falliti*, "the assembly of the bankrupts"). Florence had been invited to participate but refused. In the meantime, Borgia and his father applied to Florence for new ambassadors, who, as soon as the conspiracy was known in Florence at the beginning of October, were sent—Vittorio Soderini to Rome and Machiavelli to Borgia with instructions to preserve relations with the duke without commitment and to secure safe conduct for Florentine merchants traveling through occupied areas. On October 5 Machiavelli reached Borgia at Urbino and traveled with him to Imola on October 7. Thus began one of Machiavelli's most important legations, to last until late January 1503, during which time he would follow the duke throughout central Italy observing some of the most interesting and bizarre events of the period.

The discussions between the duke and Machiavelli focused on the former's desire to have an alliance with Florence he claimed necessary for the city because of France's support of his actions and because of the real threat to Florence posed by the rebelling captains, especially the Orsini and revenging Vitellozzo Vitelli, who continued to provoke Florence by ambiguous activity in Pisa. The duke interspersed the exchanges with warnings, threats, coaxes, and lies. Although the two men agreed on safe passage of Florentine merchants, Machiavelli successfully postponed an alliance by claiming that his lack of diplomatic authority required additional instructions from Florence. Although this upset the easily susceptible duke, his problems with the captains were more impelling. Following a defeat by the rebels of Borgia's troops led by the infamous Don Michele Coriglia, known as Don Michelotto, negotiations were established, and finally, after France agreed to supply more aid to Borgia, a settlement was reached between the duke and Orsini on October 28. Undoubtedly, the rebelling captains were intimidated by the duke's French reinforcements, the Pope's looming shadow, and their own lack of money.

The duke was a master at seeming to give important information, but in essence revealing nothing, so that Machiavelli's assigned task of keeping the *Signoria* informed was hampered by the duke's inscrutable secretiveness, deviousness, and minced words. Machiavelli did succeed in obtaining a copy of the agreement with the rebels, forwarding it to the *Dieci* on November 10 with a dispatch. His letter of October 27, 1502, reveals his insight into the hypocrisy of the agreement.[43] In his November 3 letter to the *Dieci* Machiavelli reported that the duke would avenge himself on his disloyal captains.

In the meantime, Ramiro d'Orco (de Lorqua) was charged with the administration and pacification of Romagna in early December. Although Ramiro was an avowed enemy of the rebelling Orsini, Borgia decided to have him murdered in order to dissociate himself from the cruel actions Ramiro had performed, at Borgia's request, during his brief tenure as chief agent in Romagna. On December 22 Ramiro was taken prisoner and on the twenty-third and twenty-sixth, respectively, Machiavelli tersely but vividly reported to the *Dieci* his imprisonment and cold-blooded murder.[44] This incident would exemplify a matter ". . . worthy of notice and of being copied by others. . . ," as he says in *The Prince*, 7.

The epitome of Borgia's effectiveness as a new prince—as a serpent and a basilisk—would be reflected a few days later in Sinigaglia, recently taken by Vitelli and Orsini. On December 31 the duke arrived in the city at the invitation of the captains, met with them in his quarters seemingly on a friendly basis, and then after excusing himself from the room, his soldiers burst in and arrested them. Vitelli and Oliverotto were summarily strangled that night, while the Orsini brothers were killed on January 18, 1503, since Borgia had to determine what political support the two had from their strong families in Rome.

The events in Sinigaglia occurred rapidly and resolutely with a ferocity surprising even to Machiavelli who had predicted Borgia's victory over his enemies in his November 20 and December 14 dispatches, and who had become as familiar as one could with the nondecipherable duke. Sinigaglia was the denouement of the conspiratorial drama begun at Magione, demonstrating the necessity of evil and violence within the internal, subjective logic governing the duke's political and military success. Machiavelli was summoned to the duke's quarters at 2:00 in the morning following the murders to hear of the *coup* from the perpetrator's own lips.[45]

Machiavelli's use of the word *admirato* ("wonderment") in this letter describes his reaction to the duke's revelations. The details of the episode so impressed him that he not only described them in the legation letters, but also treated them retrospectively in one of the three short discourses he wrote in 1503, *A Description of the Method Used by Duke Valentino in Killing Vitellozzo Vitelli, Oliverotto da Fermo, il signor Pagolo e il duca di Gravina Orsini*.[46] The *Description* reveals discrepancies between the version of the Sinigaglia events found there and that recorded in the legation letters. The incongruities suggest a deliberate refashioning of history which has mistakenly led some to conclude that Machiavelli was a poor historian.[47] However, the explanation is found in understanding that Machiavelli's different purposes in the two accounts reflect the Renaissance concept of history. The legation letters were intended as objective historical reports to become part of the official Chancery documents and to operate as the basis for Florentine diplomatic, political, or military action. In the *Description* Machiavelli wrote from a distance, possibly months, or years, and not as an official diplomat charged with day-to-day reporting, but rather as a historian employing a varied repertoire of literary techniques in order to project a vision transcending historical chronology. This work is, therefore, governed by a distinct literary perspective by which the events and people are modified to convey its aesthetic design, political lesson, and ethical implications.

The differences between the two versions are both obvious and subtle, evident in the facts and in the literary style. Too much emphasis on corroborating Machiavelli's factual account has resulted in neglect of his literary style. The tendency to ignore the relationship between his ideas and vision and their animating, artistic context has resulted in inaccurate or incomplete explanations of his method. This seems to be the case with the *Description*. It portrays Borgia as fearful and disarmed, alone and alienated, a point neither mentioned nor implied in the legation letters.[48] In the letters Borgia is described as arrogant, bold, and provocatory. Machiavelli's emphasis on fear and danger accentuates the duke's subsequent *virtù* in dealing with the potentially explosive situation. The duke's isolation and solitude merely underscore the genius of his autonomous military, political, and psychological conquest. Moreover, in his dealings with the rebelling captains immediately preceding the Sinigaglia episode, the *Description* portrays his actions as though betrayal unilaterally came from him rather than reciprocally from both sides. The duke's role as betrayer is heightened by his use of deception rather than open war. Machiavelli cites examples of his exploitative use of deceit and duplicity. When the captains seized Sinigaglia, the duke reveals not only his cunning, but also his quickness to score on the *occasione*. He accepts the captains' urgings to go to Sinigaglia, since the castellan of the town fortress would surrender it only to the duke. He ostensibly reassures his captains of his good faith by dismissing his much-feared French soldiers, the captains not realizing that the remaining troops would probably have sufficed to overcome them.[49] The duke then proceeds to Fano on what seems to be a journey of reconciliation and friendship.

The differences between the two accounts are further highlighted by the explanation in the *Description* of the roles played respectively by Florence and by Machiavelli during the second Borgia legation.[50] Machiavelli's instructions in the *Signoria's Commissione* were to remain neutral between Borgia and the rebelling captains until the winner could be ascertained. Machiavelli offers Florence's friendship to the duke, but never any aid or refuge. Instead, in the *Description* Machiavelli asserts that the Florentine offer of aid and asylum was in fact responsible for the duke gaining time until help could arrive. Machiavelli aggrandizes Florence's role in order to underscore her importance in the duke's decision to avenge himself. If Machiavelli intended this discourse to be included in a larger *History of Florence,* then this explanation seems all the more plausible, since he would have desired to present his city in a favorable light, especially if he wished to patronize those who might issue the commission of writing a history of Florence.

The *Description* includes elements of style and matter not appearing in the letters, further supporting the argument that Machiavelli's intention was not an exact, objective chronology of events with speculation on motives appearing only when verifiable, but instead the drawing of a verisimilar set of events, circumstances, and representative types commonly found in the politics of his age. Bondanella points out how the work is organized into five episodes or acts, as in a play,[51] suggesting a dramatic narrative structure rather than a strictly historical framework. The dramatic structure intimates at Machiavelli's playwrighting abilities to surface with *Mandragola* and *Clizia.* He also describes the geographic landscape surrounding Sinigaglia, which functions as the setting. Yet the description has more than the dramatic literary function, since it reveals the duke's *virtù* in taking advantage of Sinigaglia's strategic location—with water on the eastern side, the Apennines on the west, Borgia's reinforced troops on the north, the captains could avail themselves of only one escape from the geographically ideal trap. One can only speculate why the captains failed to perceive the duke's intentions and why they did not take measures to evade him. In the terms which govern Machiavelli's world of politics, it was a combination of their lack of *virtù* and the unavoidable course of *fortuna.*

The geographic description is preceded by an analysis of how Borgia protected against escape once the captains entered the trap. He instructs the eight men, to whom he had confided his treacherous plans, to divide into twos and to provide each captain with an escort into the quarters. This detail is never mentioned in the *Legations*. Further punctuating his precision and planning, Borgia carefully positions his soldiers strategically around the trap.

Machiavelli's method of characterization in this literary version of history suggests the beginnings of a technique which would culminate in *The Prince, The History of Florence,* and *The Life of Castruccio*. The characters of Oliverotto and especially Vitellozzo acquire dramatic strength, stature, and realism in three significant ways. First, by assuming what is essentially a third person omniscient point of view, Machiavelli is able to penetrate the characters' thoughts and provide important psychological insight, as for instance, in describing Vitellozzo's hesitancy to meet the duke at Sinigaglia. Second, Machiavelli skillfully combines this point of view with vivid visual imagery and with narrative statement of dialogue, resulting in an engrossing awareness of feelings and motives, as in the tragic description of Vitellozzo leaving his men to meet the duke, dressed in a beautiful black and green cloak complementing the pale saffron of his face, and resigned to ineludible death.[52] Vitelli's prophetically ominous departing words must have made their full impact, for when finally he is captured, his troops flee. The most dramatic and revelatory technique of characterization in the *Description* is the narrative paraphrase of the dying words of Oliverotto and Vitelli, which epitomize the symbolic historical types they represent.

The *Description* represents Machiavelli's first attempt to devise an historical method and style based on a creative adaptation of his diplomatic experiences as recorded in the *Legations*.[53] This attempt demonstrates the Renaissance connection of literary, stylistic concerns and political, historical ones. The *Description*'s political and military thesis is projected not by means of abstract maxims, but by an expressive set of literary devices and structure, or what White has called "linguistic protocols."[54] Machiavelli consolidates, redefines, and concretizes his experience of history to produce a work whose purpose and effect transcends modern scientific prerequisites of history, while still retaining its clear, precise phrasing, its impartial, detached, spectator tone. The work is dominated by the reprehensible Borgia and the ambivalent Vitellozzo, who become hypothetical constructs, imagined human types assuming universal dimensions as historical exempla. It is in this literary sense that Machiavelli "idealizes" Borgia as the personified model of the effective and necessary use of ruthlessness. It is significant that during the Borgia legation Machiavelli requested from his aid, Biagio Buonaccorsi, a copy of Plutarch's *Lives,* suggesting that at this early time he already saw the correlations between contemporary and past heroes and history.[55] Machiavelli's politics would show how universal laws were applied to successful ends by a uniquely astute and fierce individual, and specifically in the *Description* by Borgia, who is a precursor of the fuller image of the *principe nuovo* found in Machiavelli's later work.

On January 23, 1503, Machiavelli ended his second Borgia legation. Borgia returned to Rome to protect his father against those seeking to overthrow his authority. In Florence Machiavelli's Borgia dispatches were praised by the *Signoria.*[56] The historical material of the letters from this second Borgia legation would function as the basis for later adaptation, as well as providing insight into how Machiavelli's political ideas and literary style matured side by side.

In reconstructing the nature of Machiavelli's relationship with Borgia during the legation, and the evolution of his attitude toward him in his writings, six distinct sources are important: (1) the three sets of legation letters: June 1502 at Urbino, October 1502–January 1503 at Imola, and October–December 1503 at Rome; (2) the *Description;* (3) the celebrated ch. 7 of *The Prince;* (4) lines 394–96 in the 1504 *Decades,* where he refers to Borgia as the serpent and the basilisk; (5) a passage in the second brief 1503 discourse written in March, *Words to Be Spoken on the Law for Appropriating Money;* (6) and the final passage of the third discourse of 1503 written between June and August, *On the Method of Dealing with the Rebellious Peoples of the Valdichiana.* Common to these sources is Machiavelli's praise of a set of recurring qualities in his various portraits of Borgia. His personal qualities included a magnetic personality, clarity of

intellect, and strength of character. His paucity of words was punctuated by dramatic, intimidating gestures and movements. His ambition, self-confidence, audacity, and adventurousness ignited
Machiavelli's literary imagination. Borgia's determination to succeed
irrespective of scruples never evokes moral disapproval. Machiavelli
restricts his comments to Borgia's abilities as a military leader,
political strategist and administrator, and chief of state. His im-
penetrable posture and indefatigable spirit were matched if not ex-
ceeded by a rapid, target-oriented execution of carefully considered
plans and projects. The fact that Borgia granted Machiavelli so many
audiences attests to his liking of the Florentine secretary as well as
to his desire to achieve a Florentine alliance. Undoubtedly, the
second Borgia legation was a decisive event in the development of
Machiavelli's political and military ideas, historiographical style,
and literary methods.

Machiavelli's realization of the importance of papal support for
Borgia's expansionist campaign would receive its supreme verification in the fall and winter of 1503. On August 5, 1503, Pope
Alexander and his son Cesare attended a dinner with Cardinal
Adriano Corneto in his vineyard outside Rome. Soon after the Pope
and his son fell ill with malaria (Corneto was also afflicted). On
August 18, 1503, the Pope died, while Cesare struggled for life,
the malaria perhaps complicated by the effects of the later stages of
syphilis from which it is believed he suffered. Although Cesare had
anticipated his father's death, he did not expect that he, too, would
fall ill at the same time. Borgia's conquered states began to disin-
tegrate, many returning to their former lords. Pius III, old and ill,
was elected Pope, but within a month he, too, died, on October
18, and on October 23, Machiavelli was sent to Rome to observe
the election of a new Pope and the role Cesare would play in this
event. Machiavelli arrived in Rome to find that Cardinal Giuliano
della Rovere, the Borgias' bitterest enemy, was maneuvering for the
papal throne. Machiavelli's early letters from his first Rome legation
refer to the duke with some hesitancy and ambiguity, suggesting
a premonition about the duke's fate. He reports how the duke is
courted by papal aspirants, but Machiavelli's tone implies the de-
lusive nature of his hopes to influence the selection of a favorable

pope.[57] The Spanish cardinals, whom the duke ostensibly controlled, were an ambitious, avaricious lot; yet their support was crucial for any successful candidate. Giuliano della Rovere, realizing this, temporarily suspended his past enmity for the Borgias, and visited the duke, offering in return for the Spanish votes support for the duke's plan to restore the territories lost at his father's death. The duke agreed, ordering his cardinals to vote for della Rovere. The extent and nature of the promises della Rovere had made did not escape Machiavelli's scrutiny. Whether Borgia acted deliberately in taking the risk of supporting della Rovere, or whether he was duped, was uncertain, but in Machiavelli's view, he was too self-confident. The legation letters trace the progressive decline of Cesare's fortunes and along with it Machiavelli's revised opinion of him, while they show the rise of a man who would come to be known as *il Papa terribile.* Following Borgia's arrest by Julius II for failing to disclose the passwords so that the papal troops could enter the strongholds of Romagna to protect it against the attacking Venetians, he spent about five months in jail. In April 1504, he left Rome, upon his release, to fulfill the final act of his life. At thirty-two Cesare Borgia died. Some say he was killed in battle in the service of the King of Navarre, and others say he took his own life.

*Words to Be Spoken on the Law for Appropriating Money.*
The Borgia legation caused personal hardship to Machiavelli and his family. He had left home soon after his marriage promising to return in a week; instead he was gone for months, seldom writing to his wife, who constantly inquired about him at the Chancery. The family hardships were compounded by Machiavelli's less than adequate stipend and by an illness during the legation. The date for his reappointment was coming up and he had been informed that some were campaigning against him at home. On several occasions he requested recall not only because of illness, but also because he disagreed with the Florentine policy of temporizing, and because his lack of authority prohibited concrete action. When Machiavelli returned home, the experiences of the preceding months continued to influence his thinking. It is believed that in March 1503[58] he composed the short polemical discourse *Words to Be Spoken on the Law for Appropriating Money,* conceived as an imaginary speech to

be delivered by someone in authority, possibly the *gonfaloniere,* to
the *Signoria* in support of a proposal to appropriate more funds for
the military. The work, the most important of Machiavelli's minor
writings, defends the thesis of the indispensability of one's own arms
for a free, autonomous State. It is more an imaginary dialogue
between Machiavelli's persona and the Florentine *Signoria* to whom
he presents a persuasive, oratorical, and eloquent statement on their
political impotence. The work asserts the importance of combining
force with prudence to assure any government's success. The speaker
supports his deductions by past and present historical exemplification. He reminds the audience of Florence's loss of Arezzo which
should have taught the necessity of a strong military. The speaker
moves from this recent example to the generalized statement that
". . . without forces cities are not preserved but come to an
end. . . ," either destruction or servitude.[59] He counters the claims
of those who follow the middle of the road, who deny the impelling
need for arms based on the promise of France's protection or on the
belief that their enemies have no reason to attack them, with additional maxims and generalized conclusions supported with examples. He points out the domestic weaknesses created by an
unarmed, unfaithful citizenry. In addition to citizens who cower
from patriotic responsibility, Florence faces threats from France, her
apparent ally, since Florence's humiliating weaknesses inspire little
foreign esteem, and threats from Venice, whose well-known territorial ambitions had been provoked by Florence's failure to repay
loans. The most serious threat is from the incontinently ambitious
Pope and Duke Valentino, for whom private morality meant little
in the political arena where incisive, determined, and swift actions
yield positive results. The section on the delusion of depending on
another's sword is followed by a dramatically vivid slice of Byzantine
history. The speaker recalls the disastrous effects of avarice on the
irresolute citizens of Constantinople, from whom the emperor
begged money to defend the city against the attacking Turks. The
scene is accentuated by the direct quotation of the emperor's words
and by the use of sound as well as visual imagery in portraying their
regret, desolation, and tragedy. This powerful past example is juxtaposed by the exemplary actions of Valentino during his 1500

Romagna campaign. Although Machiavelli's experiences with Borgia probably resulted in the conclusions stated here, Borgia operates in this work as a figure within the larger context of Italian politics. Machiavelli suggests that Borgia's advances would have been curbed if Florence had been prepared. He recalls the image of the *gonfaloniere* who as he reported the loss of Faenza ". . . wept over your unbelief and obstinacy and forced you to have mercy on yourselves,"[60] thus comparing him to the Emperor of Constantinople.

Machiavelli's method of historical exemplification in defending his appeal for force, independence, and swift action is enhanced by an impatient tone of exhortation and recrimination. The often derisive, abusive observations are expressed in sentences whose rhythm is emphatically, almost hypnotically repetitive in syntax and parallel in structure. The piece ends with the observation that Fortune is only with those who arm themselves and who clearly understand the need for change in changing times.

*On the Method of Dealing with the Rebellious Peoples of the Valdichiana.* The Valdichiana uprising again demonstrated Florence's inept political policy.[61] Valdichiana and Arezzo rebelled on June 4, 1502, and it was only because of France's intervention that the rebelling peoples were reconquered in August of the same year. Although the rebellion was provoked by the avenging and conspiratorial Vitellozzo Vitelli, who claimed the cities in the name of Piero de' Medici (even though in fact he was one of Borgia's captains), the incident demonstrated how Florence had failed to unify her territories. In his short piece on the rebellious people of Valdichiana Machiavelli treats how a government can assure control of its subjects. The date usually assigned to the work is 1503, specifically between June 1 and August 18, because of Machiavelli's reference in the work to the events in Arezzo and Valdichiana as occurring "last year" and the allusion in the final lines that Pope Alexander VI was not yet dead.[62] Like the other two short discourses believed composed in 1503, it has a distinct literary quality combined with an analogical use of past history, specifically Livy, to support political maxims. Like the other two, the Valdichiana discourse was not motivated by his official Chancery duties and the point of view is markedly retrospective and evaluative. Machiavelli's use of historical example is punctuated by a prose style employing "either-or" contraposition. His advice on the dangerous consequences of following a middle of the road policy, as Florence seems to have done in dealing with the rebellious citizens, is based on his notion, for the first time here expressed, of the immutability of human passions. This psychological fact demands that history be the model for political actions. The problem of Florence's rebelling citizens was complicated at that time by the Borgian threat. Borgia's role exemplifies how contemporary history required that Florence be decisive and resolute and how the imponderable vagaries of Fortuna demanded that Cesare take immediate steps against Florence, while he could still count on papal support.

A tripartite structure is clearly evident in the Valdichiana discourse. Part I describes the Roman historical analogy which for Machiavelli, the humanist, assumes modern relevance; part II critiques Florence's actions in Arezzo and Valdichiana, implicitly contrasting them with the Roman example; part III exhorts and warns how the Borgian threat necessitated the adoption of determined, effective political policy. Part I begins by recalling an event from Roman history, the speech of Lucio Furio Camillo to the Senate on how the conquered peoples of Lazio should be treated to secure against further rebellion. Camillo's advice, that conquered rebels must be treated decisively, either fully benefited to gain their loyalty or destroyed to avoid future uprisings, functions as an inductive springboard for Machiavelli's subsequent generalizations. Ambiguity or halfway measures suspending people between hope and fear must be avoided. The policy of punishment or reward should, however, be applied on a specific, case-by-case basis. The Senate decided that circumstances warranted the Lanuvins be made Roman citizens, as were the Aricins, Nomentans, Pedans, Tusculans, while the Veliterns were cruelly castigated and their city burned, since despite their ancient Roman citizenship, they had rebelled many times. The people of Anzio were also punished. New inhabitants were sent to Anzio to overwhelm the old, their ships were taken away, and they were prohibited from building others. Thus, Roman policy was to benefit those they hoped to reconcile, and punish those whose fidelity they could never earn. The Romans employed two methods when peoples had to be treated cruelly: (1) their city could be ruined and whatever inhabitants remained would be sent to Rome to live, or (2) new inhabitants would be sent to live in the rebelling city to overwhelm the old.

Part II begins with the deductive proposition that history is the teacher of our actions based on the continuity of human passions. The Roman precedent demonstrates that in all times there is he who commands and he who serves; he who serves willingly and he who does not. The principle was seen to operate in Florence's relationship with Arezzo, whose citizens could be compared to the Veliterns or the Anzians, but who Florence did not treat similarly. Machiavelli shows how the Aretines had been neither fully benefited nor fully destroyed and that such halfway measures with Florence's continued mismanagement of Arezzo had caused continued discontent and eventual rebellion.

Part III dramatizes Borgia's threat looming over Florence and her badly organized and administered territorial possessions. Machiavelli points out how he never depended on Italian friendships to maintain his conquered lands. He turned neither to Venice nor to Florence, indicating expansionist designs on these republics; instead he depended on foreign assistance. Machiavelli, through his speaking persona, reminds the audience of once having heard Cardinal Francesco Soderini, his companion during the first Borgia legation, say that the Pope and his duke, among their other praiseworthy political qualities, understood the importance of seizing the opportunity, or avoiding hesitancy, of thinking while in motion, and of acting swiftly. It seemed predictable to Machiavelli that the duke would soon act to effect his aspirations on Tuscany since he was well aware of the Pope's advancing age.

Although the piece lacks the dramatic vividness of the *Description* or the powerful impact of the *Words,* it boasts a tightness of organic structure and a skillful adaptation of ancient history to contemporary circumstances. The subtle comparison of Camillo, the clever Roman general and consul who conquered the rebelling peoples and who understood how to rule them, to Borgia, a potential Camillo, solidifies the structural unity. The reverberations of Camillo's speech are felt in Italy in Borgia's actions. Foiling both is the insipience of Florentine methods. Machiavelli's technique intimates the direct, frank, definitive, and realistic manner, without moral evaluation, especially characteristic of *The Prince*. The unqualified swiftness and resoluteness he advocates is brilliantly imitated in his prose style; his radicalized juxtaposition of available alternatives is projected in clauses or phrases evolving from a lucidly defined "either-or" structure which finds its source and model in Camillo's very words. The importance of the Valdichiana discourse resides in how Machiavelli (1) carefully establishes an organic literary relationship among the elements of structure, style, and content; (2) introduces a psychological basis to buttress his political ideas; (3) uses the impelling universality of man's nature to justify and authenticate the relevance of past history to a modern context.

## Chapter Two
# Politics, History, and Literature in *The Prince*

## Composition, Dedication, and Structure

In his December 10, 1513, letter to his friend Francesco Vettori, then Florentine ambassador to Rome, Machiavelli describes his days in exile, seven miles from Florence on his small rural estate at Sant' Andrea in Percussina.[1] Following his removal from office, imprisonment, and torture, Machiavelli was forced to withdraw from politics, but he continued to evaluate the meaning of his fifteen years of political experiences and their relationship to the solution of contemporary problems and to the universal flow of history. He began a treatise on republics which would, after several interruptions and revisions, become the *Discourses*. That Machiavelli should have been inspired to comment on the virtues of republican government was consistent with his family background, political experience, and personal preference, yet in this same letter he informs his friend that he had interrupted his commentary on the ancients to write a little work *(uno opuscolo)* entitled *De principatibus* [On Princedoms]. Why Machiavelli shifted from republics to principalities can only be speculated in light of what he says in the letter as to why he wrote this *ghiribizzo* ("fantasy"). From what is known of his personal wealth, his comments on his own poverty were not exaggerated. Financial need as well as a desire to return to public life undoubtedly inspired his shift from speculative theorizing about republics to practical advice on princedoms intended to procure him a position in the new Medici government. Stylistically and thematically *The Prince* reflects his intention to have the work applied in contemporary Italian politics. He recognized that the nature of the Italian and Florentine political climate required extraordinary and uncommon practices not otherwise acceptable to him in view of his republican sentiments.

Machiavelli turned to the writing of *The Prince* at that point in his writing of the *Discourses*, I, 17 and 18, when he discusses how, when a corrupt people attains freedom, it has the greatest difficulty in maintaining it, and how free government can be maintained in corrupt cities, if it is already there, and if it is not there, how it can be established. In considering the example of the contemporary Italian states, he concludes in *Discourses* I, 17 that the revival of good laws in a corrupt city or state can be achieved only by abnormal, extralegal methods employed by an exceptional leader notable for his *virtù*—a conclusion which seems to be the springboard for *The Prince*.[2] That the *Discourses* were begun before *The Prince* is verified at the beginning of ch. 2 of *The Prince:* "I shall omit discussing republics because elsewhere I have discussed them at length." The most accepted view is that Machiavelli composed it between July and December 1513, and that it did not undergo any revision after that time.[3]

Although Machiavelli intended to dedicate and present *The Prince* to Giuliano de' Medici, the younger brother of Pope Leo X, to whom Machiavelli attributed his release from prison, he delayed and then it was too late, for Giuliano died on March 17, 1516. Upon his death, Giuliano's nephew, the twenty-one-year-old Lorenzo, was elected captain general of the Florentines in May 1516, and on October 8, 1516, he became Duke of Urbino following the capture of that city. Sometime between May and October 1516 Machiavelli wrote the dedicatory letter to Lorenzo.[4] Legend has it that Lorenzo ignored *The Prince,* more interested in a handsome pair of greyhounds presented to him at the same time.

The dedication defines Machiavelli's ostensible intention and stylistic approach in *The Prince.* It has traditionally shocked its readers, not so much for the novelty of ideas, but rather for the unequivocal statement of distasteful concepts which others had often camouflaged or dignified by copious eloquence. Treatises on the education of a prince, known as *de regimine principum,* were commonplace in political literature before Machiavelli, as exemplified by the writings of Colonna, Pontano, Platina, Patrizi, Carafa, Biondo, among others.[5]

Machiavelli's practical intention is further supported by his choice of the vernacular rather than Latin, common to orthodox humanistic treatises in this genre. He saw himself both as an imitator and an innovator of the genre. Although in the earliest manuscripts of *The Prince,* Latin chapter headings appear, in Machiavelli's final review of the work apparently accomplished just before his death, he changed them to Italian.

Machiavelli's uniqueness in *The Prince* derives greatly from his departure from the typical idealization of the prince into a figure living only in the writer's fantasy. In the dedication Machiavelli seems to reject the resources of elocution and rhetoric characteristic of the magniloquent Ciceronian prose style. In some ways he anticipates Bacon's rejection in the *Advancement of Learning,* I (1605) of the style which emphasized words rather than matter. Judging it detrimental to the progress of learning, Bacon defined the affected style of eloquence and copiousness which demanded choice phrases, rounded sentences, tropes and figures.[6] Machiavelli's definition of his style in the dedication sounds like a paraphrase of Bacon. The dedication previews the typical movement of his prose in *The Prince,* from the generalized, deductive, often aphoristic statement to the concrete, specific, and personal example, as for instance, in sentences one and two of the first paragraph of the dedication which leap from the abstract to concrete. The third sentence extends the specificity of the second by rendering it more personal in referring to the writer's understanding of great men, in his recognition of the educative role of history, in his recourse to empirical observation, direct and vicarious experience. His seemingly self-effacing manner is countered by his didactic intention and utilitarian motive, ". . . to give you the means for learning. . . ." Like Bacon, he expresses concern that an affected eloquence will impede the clear communication of the knowledge he possesses about political matters, knowledge gained experientially, empirically, and through historical study, which he hopes the new prince can use to beneficial ends. Yet the emphasis on matter rather than words does not result in a less diligent prose style; it is a plain style dedicated to truthful content (*verità effettuale*) no matter how shocking or unpleasant. Machiavelli's experience and knowledge require in his view the abandonment of predetermined forms in the formulation of an appropriately expressive prose style.

Additional characteristics distinguish Machiavelli's anticopious style. Shifting unexpectedly from the literal to the poetic or metaphorical, he climaxes his dedication with an extended analogy, or prose conceit. The prince's perspective from atop his high mountain of power and authority makes him an astute observer of the people, while they who occupy the low and humble valleys may have a clearer perspective of the prince. The dedication reveals the sententiousness, wit, and skepticism typical of Machiavelli's prose. Its terseness, paralleled word patterns, and sentence structure fulfill Bacon's aim of tracing the movement of the inquiring, scientific mind. Although the distinctive aspects of his style convey the effect of laborious, analytical inquiry intended to discover and communicate the truth, Machiavelli does not, as the English seventeenth-century prose writers such as Bacon would not, abandon a continuity with the older prose manner. One of his hallmarks is his citation of classical authority and his advocacy of imitation, both of which link him to the conceptual and practical aims of Renaissance humanism. Yet little has been done to relate Machiavelli to the development of a new prose style in Europe and even less attention has been paid to a comparative study of how he contributed to the emergence of a scientific prose style as advanced by Bacon, Montaigne, and others in the late seventeenth century. Machiavelli shares its contradictory, paradoxical, and colloquial manner, its use of attention-getting devices, variant repetition of the central idea, its immediacy and irregular syntax.

As with most Renaissance dedications to treatises on the education of the prince, the dedication to *The Prince* flatters the patron, announces the subject, defines the approach, and establishes the author's authority. The chapters of *The Prince* can be conveniently divided into four major sections:[7] chs. 1 through 11 deal with the types of principates in ancient and contemporary history and how they are gained by force, favorable circumstances, wicked deeds, or favor of the citizens; chs. 12 through 14 deal with the prince's use of the army—mercenary, national, and auxiliary—in maintaining his principate; chs. 15 through 23 give specific advice on the qualities of a successful new prince and those qualities of *virtù* which assure effective reign over the people; chs. 24 through 26 apply the previous precepts to Italy, explaining why Italian princes lost their states, and exhorting the addressee to free Italy from foreign barbarians.

The structure of *The Prince* has been an important question because of the seeming dissimilarity in tone and style between the last chapter and the rest of the work. The stylistic qualities of this chapter will be discussed in a later section; however, let us include at this point some general comments about the twenty-sixth chapter. The patriotic nationalism of the final chapter is not inconsistent with what occurs previously, nor is its heightened rhetorical and lyrical quality. It was not uncommon for political and ethical treatises to include an exhortative section appealing to the reader for agreement and concerted action. Its emotional and poetical qualities are found in numerous places elsewhere in *The Prince*. The work as a whole is replete with cross-references and allusions to other sections, in the form of characters and events, some of which appear in the final chapter. When viewed within the context of the entire work, the twenty-sixth chapter reflects Machiavelli's consistent mingling of the objective and scientific with the emotional and aesthetic, and in this sense he was no different from most Renaissance artists. At times he is the methodical, detached, anatomizing scientist, while at others he is the discursive, emotionally committed artist. Yet at all times he is aware of the work's unifying idea, structure, and purpose; his summary statements and reiterative comments at strategic points throughout the work testify to this fact. Neither the scientist nor the artist, however, can or should be inhibited by that single focus from exploring any area of possible relationship, and certainly in the Renaissance there were few of the modern distinctions between science and art. The problem of whether *The Prince* is a unified work can ultimately be resolved only by a careful study of its overall stylistic qualities, and not by the contextual isolation of any one part.

## The New Prince as a Mythic Hero

Although Machiavelli acknowledges the hereditary principality, his chief concern, the new princedom and the new kind of leader it would demand, operates as the force coalescing *The Prince*'s political and aesthetic elements. As a specific type of book inspired by a specific situation and linked directly to its own age, it requires an informing knowledge of contemporary history. Yet, it has generated a universal interest transcending Renaissance boundaries. To a great extent this results from Machiavelli's portrayal of the new Prince, which blends the qualities of the historical, literary, and mythic definitions of hero. The new Prince as ideal hero is an exceptional military and political leader and role-model, with outstanding intelligence, will, and discipline. He possesses commanding authority, vigorous but controlled passions, and unusual abilities of expression. Like the literary hero, his greatness lies in what he is, in the praiseworthy qualities he objectifies, but also like the historical hero, his greatness derives from what he does and how those actions are performed, his *virtù* and *modo di procedere* ("manner of acting").[8] Unlike the literary hero, he does not project the nobility of character inherent to the Christian virtues, but in his rule he must show such discipline and selflessness as to protect him from outright moral condemnation. The successful political heroes Machiavelli cites as his paragons—Moses, Cyrus, Theseus, and Romulus—had learned how to use the power to be not good in accordance with occasion and necessity. As men of government ignoring self-interest, they were dedicated to the stability, security, independence, strength, and glory of the societies they led. They learned how not to be virtuous and to resort to evil means to accomplish the political goals of power and greatness for the common good. In emulating the actions of these mythic armed prophets, Machiavelli's hero must, like them, function as a scapegoat, as a surrogate willing to risk potential death, both spiritual and physical, for he must sacrifice the private morality which would save his soul in return for the public good. This archetypal quality associates him with the mythic hero, while his characteristic use of deception and fraud shows him as a serious version of the mythic trickster exemplified so well in the personality of Odysseus. The new Prince synthesizes the qualities epitomized by individual heroes from Homer to the Renaissance—the *arete* of a courageous, wise, and eloquent Achilles; the adventurous, clever spirit of an Odysseus; the *pietas* of a morally committed, ever-responsible Aeneas; the *sapientia et fortitudo* of a Roland; the harmonious blending of arms and studies typical of Castiglione's ideal Renaissance courtier.[9] What transforms him, however, from simple literary *topos,* or historical *exemplum,* into a mythic archetype is the macrocosmic, transcendental value Machiavelli assigns to his hero-task—his mission is to regenerate Italian civil life. Italy had become like all corrupted states incapable of regaining order and stability without the leadership of this Savior man who would employ extreme measures (*debiti mezzi,* "suitable means") to reanimate and redirect its political and social course toward the common good.

His individuality, solitariness, and isolation, qualities which can anachronistically be termed "gothic," further link him to the hallmarks of the traditional mythic archetype of the hero. It is only as a sole ruler that he can establish the discipline and absolute authority needed for a stable, enduring new state. The undiffused force of a unique, self-sufficient leader excelling others is a prerequisite both for the founding of an integrated state where none previously existed, as reflected in the heroic missions of Romulus and Cyrus, or for its reconstruction after a period of decline and corruption. He is a leader who understands what Zarathustra[10] well expressed, that man is a rope tied between beast and oberman, and that life is often more dangerous among men than among animals. He is trained and equipped in the two ways of fighting: by law and the ways of man, and by force and the ways of beasts. *The Prince,* 18 presents a memorable analysis of how the new prince must act in certain circumstances by recalling the mythical figure of Chiron, the Centaur, the purported teacher of Achilles. Typically, Machiavelli supports his generalized deductions with examples, but here they assume brilliantly imaginative dimensions that exceed mere historical citation. The image not only acts as *exemplum* supporting his assertion that from ancient times leaders were trained to use selectively the traits of animal and of man in securing political permanence, but it also affirms his endorsement of classical heroism as relevant to his own age. The new prince must amalgamate the cunning of the fox to recognize traps with the force of the lion to frighten wolves, and the rationality of human intelligence to evaluate information if he hopes to achieve endurance and stability for his state and fame and glory for himself.[11]

Machiavelli's concern for the qualities and role of the new prince—an upstart, often usurping leader who comes to power through his own ability and army, through fortune and someone else's army, or through evil deeds—seemed motivated by the plans known in 1513 to establish Giuliano de' Medici as a new prince. It was hoped that by good government he would win the affection and loyalty of his subjects, expand from that state, and eventually, like Machiavelli's model of Theseus who freed the Athenians of the Minotaur and united the peoples of Attica, expel foreign invaders and gain independence for Italy.[12] The analogy of Theseus seemed appropriate, for the new prince must conquer a symbolic monster and unite the disparate Italian cities and territories into a single ethnic unit. Although the new prince was a political phenomenon abounding in Italy at the end of the fifteenth century and the beginning of the sixteenth, few if any seemed able to resolve Italy's problems on a peninsular scale. This new political leader, who would assert his *mano regia,* seemed justified in light of the chaotic Italian situation and the history of Florentine internal dissension and instability. Machiavelli's political vision was inspired by this crisis to consider what positive role this new kind of leader could play in redeeming, restoring, and unifying Italy.

*The Prince,* chs. 15–23, lists the qualities of this savior, the methods to use in various circumstances, and the nature of his relationship to those he ruled—what he could expect and demand and how he should use them to achieve his ends. Although he must appear virtuous, he should not ". . . worry about incurring reproach for those vices without which he can hardly maintain his position. . . ,"[13] including when necessary avarice, cruelty, breaking of promises, and the abandonment of conventional ethics. Hatred by the new subjects must be avoided, but it would be safer for him to be feared than loved, for there are times, as with Moses, Cyrus, Romulus, and Theseus, when wise cruelty is true mercy. Scipio exemplifies that excessive mercy and liberality are fatal to the new prince, yet cruelty motivated by malevolence, misunderstanding, or revenge, or cruelty not inspired by the welfare of the state is unacceptable, for although as with Agathocles, it may assist in establishing power and effective rule, it could not be called noble nor would it bring glory to the perpetrator.

### *Virtù* and *Fortuna* in *The Prince*[14]

In utilizing the qualities of the lion and the fox the new prince must exhibit *virtù*. Translators attempting to define Machiavelli's term have often distorted, misapplied, or misunderstood his meaning in a specific context. The word derives from the Latin, *virtus,* meaning "courage" or "valor." Eluding reducibility to a single comprehensive meaning, Machiavelli's concept of *virtù* extends beyond this synonym and though synonyms are useful in arriving at a readable translation, we must always have its complex ramifications along with its specific context in mind. Though not exhaustive, the list of possible synonyms includes: ability, force, courage, boldness, efficiency, energy, vitality, wisdom, capacity, power, action, valor, strength, bravery, self-discipline, determination, fortitude, prudence. Among the English words which this list should not include is "virtuous," meaning morally good, since Machiavelli ordinarily did not mean any Christian, or even classical sense of moral goodness; in fact, his concept is opposite to the contemplation inherent in the Christian idea of virtue. He believed that Christian asceticism impeded social and political progress by encouraging men to endure suffering rather than to rebel against tyrannous and subjugating systems. *Virtù* conveys a sense of energetic, active, conscious involvement in determining the political, civic, and military life of the state. In the sense that *virtù* opposes passivity, it is anti-Christian; otherwise it transcends conventional goodness or badness; yet the constructive use of energy for good ends is preferred to its evil use for wicked ends. In swift, effective action the new prince can successfully convert his will into reality and affix his mark on history. His will is neither arbitrary nor capricious, but clearly aware of the possibilities and opportunities inherent in a situation and capable of utilizing all resources in translating thought into action.

Important to *virtù* is the ability to understand, accept, and adapt
to change dynamically and avoid stagnation. *Necessità* and *occasione*
are significant, for the exigencies presented by the conditions of an
occasion may demand specific action. As Machiavelli dramatically
points out in *The Prince, 26,* it was necessary that the Israelites be
enslaved for Moses to show his ability, for the Persians to be discontent for Cyrus to be great, for the Athenians to be scattered for
Theseus to lead them. Machiavelli finds the same conditions of
necessity—enslavement, servitude, disunity, leaderlessness—exist-
ing in his contemporary Italy. The degree to which a new prince
can take advantage of the apparently negative or contrary elements
of an occasion and channel them toward a successful end depends
on his perception of the real nature of things *(realtà effettuale).*

It is at this point that Machiavelli's concept of *fortuna* enters as
an irrational force sometimes beyond men's control. *Fortuna,* like
*virtù,* has its own contextual meanings. At times it might mean
God, or the heavens, or just luck, but in general it means the
voluble, unstable vicissitudes of the human condition. *Fortuna* provides the opportunity *(occasione)* to demonstrate *virtù;* its impermanence requires prompt action which may or may not succeed
since *fortuna* is willful, arbitrary, impersonal, and indiscriminate.
It ignores traditional concepts of justice or of moral rectitude. In
fathoming the vacillations of *fortuna,* the new prince must struggle
not only against the contrary conditions of the occasion, but also
his own inescapable limitations and the inevitable and universal
processes of decay. *Fortuna* and *virtù* dialectically collide as he grap-
ples to control unpredictable events, to seize the fleeting opportunity, to minimize unavoidable decline, to maximize the force of his
will, to turn to his advantage conditions and realities for which he
is not responsible, in essence, to synthesize the opposing fields of
*virtù* and *fortuna.*

It is in politics and war that Machiavelli dramatically portrays
the encounter of *virtù* with *fortuna.* The dynamism, strength, and
heroism of the man of action, who displays *grandezza d'animo* ("greatness of soul") and *fortezza di corpo* ("strength of body"), are epitomized
in the great political and military leader who founds a new state or
regenerates a corrupt and declining one. Actual war or warlike

circumstances (since politics is a kind of battle where battlefield conditions often prevail) are the supreme test of his *virtù,* of the leadership qualities fundamental to the struggle against *fortuna.* These concepts do not remain theoretical, since Machiavelli provides numerous examples of successful and unsuccessful "warriors" of *virtù.*[15]

Machiavelli's most complete discussion of *fortuna* in *The Prince* appears in ch. 25, where he affirms the role of man's free will in turning to his advantage at least one half of all actions. In stressing the need to forestall the variations of *fortuna,* Machiavelli resorts to the prose conceit of the analogous situation of preparing for the possibility of floods. Preparation, foresight, and flexibility are essential to assure that actions are suited to the times. Machiavelli cites Pope Julius II as an example of how a man successfully adapted his innate impetuousity to the circumstances, but he warns that future conditions may have required methods inconsistent with Julius's nature. This chapter ends with the memorable conceit personifying *fortuna* as a capricious, shrewish woman who must be beaten into submission. In advocating his preference for impetuosity over cautiousness, he concludes that *fortuna* is more friendly to the less cautious, more spirited young.

*Fortuna-virtù* applies collectively to the people of a state as well as to leaders. Nations, like people, possess political and military energy. Just as education shapes and cultivates the qualities of *virtù* innate to the new prince, likewise social and political education, structure, and discipline shapes and cultivates a people's *virtù.* Necessity, such as war, hard times, or other catastrophes, can, depending on their *virtù,* either destroy or redeem a people. Civic corruption, neglect of military obligations, lack of discipline, order, and organization will impair a people's ability to cope with the necessity of occasions in their historical evolution. *Virtù* transcends time and individuals, even though it is concretized in specific historical moments and human figures. A state's dynamic progress, the fulfillment of its unique historical function, its ability to achieve liberty, peace, stability, and endurance, depends on the *virtù* of its citizens and its leader. Paradoxically, here Machiavelli's republican sentiments and monarchical tendencies coalesce. He recognizes that a strong, stable, and enduring republic could never emerge without the great individual leader, the heroic, audacious man of action. Yet the people's *virtù* would ultimately determine whether the republic, once established, after a period of monarchical rule would prevail.

The figure who more than any other in *The Prince* objectifies the dynamics of *virtù* and *fortuna* is Cesare Borgia. Machiavelli's focus on Borgia in ch. 7 prevents his portrait of the new prince from remaining an abstract and ideal construct of his fantasy. It affirms that this concept of a warlike statesman could in fact become an historical reality; the image of the possible is transformed into the actual. Borgia epitomizes how *virtù*—his calculation, poise, determined will, and resolute effectuation of political and military goals—collides with inscrutable, unpredictable, and malicious *fortuna*. The prince who rises from the people with little experience in public life and no power base will face innumerable difficulties. Borgia exemplifies the private citizen who ". . . gained his position through his father's Fortune and through her lost it. . . ."[16] The Medici addressee should imitate the Borgia example in how a new prince acquires and builds a "mixed state," and eventually, as proposed in ch. 26, uses the new state to thrust out the foreign invaders of Italy.[17] Although Borgia followed all the rules, however, *fortuna*— the untimely death of his father, his own sickness, and his miscalculation in supporting the papal candidacy of Julius II—brought his downfall. Borgia demonstrates how a new ruler who generally acted with *virtù* in founding a new state is overcome by the exercise of bad judgment—in supporting a candidate for pope who feared and despised him. In the most critical moment of his struggle to build a new state, the prince is abandoned by *fortuna*.

## The Function of History

Machiavelli says in *The Prince,* 7 that Borgia's actions are an example ". . . worthy of notice and of being copied by others. . . ." The doctrine of imitation, fundamental to Machiavelli's political theories and to his concept of the function of history, imbues it with a comprehensiveness approaching the poetical, mythical, and even ritualistic. A more thorough discussion of Machiavelli's view of history occurs later in this book (ch. 5); however, let us mention

how his theory is reflected in *The Prince* and how it defines his
approach to the rule by a new prince.

At the beginning of ch. 6, Machiavelli states the importance of
imitating the actions of great men, a statement whose significance
extends beyond the limits of his discussion of new princedoms gained
through a man's own armies and ability—the specific subject of ch.
6. It defines the criteria he uses to evaluate political action in a
particular set of circumstances. The prudent new prince will follow
the ". . . paths beaten by great men and . . . imitate those who
have been especially admirable. . . ."[18] In expressing this idea
Machiavelli employs a stylistic device which imitates the concept;
the analogy of the prudent archer who aims higher than his mark.
The analogy objectifies the function of imitation and the presence
of internal correspondences in the historical events of various periods.
The statement displays aspects typical of the relationship of Machiavelli's style and thought to Renaissance literary theory and practice. He alludes to the humanistic notion of the didactic function
of classical allusions, both pagan and Christian. Imitation also included the citation of common sense wisdom and the tested empirical
evidence of experience epitomized in proverbs and popular sayings,
such as, "He who builds on the people builds on mud" (ch. 9). The
emulation of paragons can be compared to a similar practice among
the literary and artistic masters of the time. The resurrection of the
heroic deeds of legendary and historical men, especially Romans,
along with the Renaissance's affinity for the past suggests the humanists' moral and educative mission. Machiavelli states (ch. 14)
that the prudent new prince trains his mind by reading the histories
of excellent men such as Achilles, who was imitated by Alexander;
Alexander, who was imitated by Caesar; Cyrus, who was imitated
by Scipio; etc. The practical humanists believed that the resource
book of the past offered a moral paradigm which would stimulate
present action. The study of the past not only legitimized the present, but the discovery of the absolute laws of man's existence would
reconcile the strains of idealism and realism inherent to humanistic
ethic. It avoided the abstractions of scholasticism by embodying its
conceptual ideals in living, vibrant images.

Machiavelli's dialectic with the remote and immediate past extends from objective history to personal history or experience as well. *L'esperienza delle cose moderne* ("the experience of modern things"), the lessons of 200 years of Italian history, and especially those more recent in which he played some role, are likewise sublimated into his political and historical thought. The modern examples offered during his years in public life merely illuminate and confirm the universal techniques and rules he cites in *The Prince.* His involvement in the making of contemporary history as a Florentine diplomatic envoy combines with his tendency to idealize, especially when dealing with Roman or Florentine history. This has caused some modern critics to view him prematurely as a bad historian, a biased proselyte at times, and prejudiced denigrator at others. Machiavelli's approach can perhaps best be described as *metahistorical,*[19] whereby he weaves between the realms of history and poetry (*poetry* used here in the Renaissance sense of artistic literature which includes prose as well as poetry) with the distinctions between the two forms of "knowledge" often noticeably blurred. He does what historians are supposed to do—verbally imitating an action or event and making assertions about its meaning—and he also does what poets do—employing images, symbols, and other literary and rhetorical devices. He constructs a verisimilar set of typical and recurring events, people, and circumstances, often deviating from fact or only partially approximating fact, and whose source is not strictly verifiable by a specific external model.[20] In citing the prototypes of Moses, Theseus, Cyrus, and Romulus alongside the contemporary Savonarola, King Ferdinand, and Borgia, Machiavelli affirms the recurrence of similar political figures and situations in the tide of history. They function like pantomime characters in a dramatic performance whose symbolic identity the audience would easily recognize.[21] Consequently, Machiavelli's literary approach to history cannot always be judged by the truth of what he says about an historical happening or by the congruence of his interpretation with the original model. His historical consciousness is permeated by a "mystique-sense."[22] The historical events defining the heroic achievements of Machiavelli's models, as well as those of his new prince who emulates them, have assumed a transcendental, all-encompassing value, exceeding the limits of their historical period. Machiavelli as mythmaker exemplifies the process of *mythopoesis* ("fabulation" or, as he called it, *ghiribizzo*) at work; the historical exemplars are the armed prophets of their respective ages; for others they are called shamans or medicine men who diagnosed, treated, and healed; and for even others they are the rope-dancers who eluded the deadly abyss. Elements of both the primitive medicine man and of Nietzsche's *Ubermensch* ("oberman" or "superman") are reflected in Machiavelli's *mythomorph*[23] of the new prince, but without their fanatical disequilibrium and egotism.

Machiavelli's view of history relates to his view of man as a social and political being. At the beginning of ch. 15 in one of those important statements appearing at crucial points throughout *The Prince* in which Machiavelli summarizes what has come before and then announces the subject, states his purpose, and defines his approach for the subsequent section, he affirms a view of man basic not only to *The Prince,* but to all his writings. After remarking on his methodological originality and reaffirming his desire ". . . . to write something useful to him who comprehends it . . . ," Machiavelli notes that the moral constrictions governing how men ought to live have nothing in common with the reality of how men do in fact live. Acting in accord with those moral constrictions among so many who are not good will assure the new prince's destruction. Later (ch. 17) he specifies how men are bad. Although it would be desirable for the new prince to be both loved and feared, it is safer to be feared than loved because since men are evil and do not hesitate to injure one who is loved, they can be intimidated from evil by fear of punishment. Throughout *The Prince* Machiavelli employs this view of man to justify the new prince's use of methods which would otherwise be considered immoral from a Judeo-Christian ethical perspective. Yet he is speaking of man only as a social and political entity, as observed in action and in history, and is not describing man's metaphysical or spiritual condition.[24] Machiavelli's concept of history relates to his view of man, for it documents his ambition, greed, and envy as motives in historical events. Machiavelli finds that the baseness of man's passions in society and politics is unalterably consistent throughout all peoples, in all nations, and in all times, and that it can determine the outcome of political action, and in fact, the survival or destruction of a people. The discrepancy between the private, spiritual doctrines which dictate how man *ought* to live and the way he actually lives in his public life prompts Machiavelli to reject the idealistic and fantastical works on this subject and to assert that he will deal with the truth. Some have tried to see in Machiavelli's seemingly negative view of man a quality of Christian pessimism, possibly equating it with St. Augustine's notion of man's corrupted nature, with Machiavelli substituting *virtù* for Augustine's requisite of grace.[25] Although grace and *virtù* do redeem man, Machiavelli's concern in *The Prince* was to study man's civic behavior and to arrive at practical rules of action for the new Renaissance prince which would assure the state's political health, stability, and longevity by forcing man to adhere to laws beneficial to its collective welfare, and impede him from maximizing personal, selfish gain. Thus, the study of history not only exemplifies the ineffectiveness of previous political action and provides positive models of behavior to be imitated in certain political situations for present and future success, but it also authenticates an unequivocal declaration about man's corrupt nature which demonstrates why those past rulers succeeded or failed.

## Morality, Ethics, and Religion in *The Prince*

Machiavelli's pessimistic view of man requires closer consideration of the morality of many of his political axioms. This point, perhaps more than any other, has consistently inspired controversy among his antagonists and apologists. The shocking effect of many of his maxims emanates from his seeming perversion, or inversion, of the ethical principles which the traditional Judeo-Christian mythological archetypes validate as applicable to man's public as well as his private life. Machiavelli's modernism derives from his apparent challenge of the myth of the ". . . privilege of race and its concept of an eternally valid moral law divinely delivered to the privileged race from the summit of Mount Sinai. . . ."[26] The consequence of his political mythology, which subtly and ironically undermines established religious myths institutionalized into politics, is to provide a surrogate for conventional ethics specifically in man's public actions as a leader, politician, and statesman. This new order, unlike the old from which it derives, is no longer judged as an ultimate goal; but as an instrument in achieving a politicized, mythic view of society and man's place in it. The figures and mythic symbols personifying the ancient laws, Moses, for example, reappear, but transformed by a radically altered concept of cosmology and social order shaped by a chiefly political and social, rather than religious, vision.

Machiavelli's contemporaries and immediate successors were not always shocked or enraged, as were some later critics, by the apparent immorality of the actions he encouraged the new prince to follow. Many seemed to understand both the literary origins and the political, social, and diplomatic history which the work described and by which it had been provoked. Terrorism, murder, cruelty, treachery, and military aggression to achieve political ends were, however, no more common in Renaissance times than today, nor was Machiavelli the first to advocate them, evidences of which can be found in Aristotle and Cicero, among others. Moreover, it would be a mistake to think that either Machiavelli personally was immoral, as has so often been suggested in the misapplication of the word "machiavellian," or that in his analysis of politics he ignored ethical ideals. A careful reading of those passages in *The Prince* often exerpted as demonstrating Machiavelli's immorality suggests the opposite. For instance, in ch. 15, following his statement that he is concerned with how men live and not how they ought to live, he lists the virtues and vices which often bring praise or blame. Acknowledging that virtue—mercy, faith, integrity, humanity, etc.—would obviously be more desirable, he also recognizes that "human conditions . . . do not always permit it . . ." because men are not all good.[27] Machiavelli recognizes the crucial role of appearance in fruitful political action, for the ". . . mob is always fascinated by appearances and . . . in the world the mob is everything."[28]

Machiavelli discriminates between the ideals and values governing the private life of the prince and those governing his public life. Just as Christian moral values dictate ethical action in man's private, spiritual life, so too the techniques of politics dictate certain kinds of action in the leader's public life. The common good and public realm must have priority, and although the prince should wherever possible follow ethics even in politics, his responsibility as leader demands he be ready to abandon it, and even the salvation of his soul, if constrained by political necessity. Evil committed or prolonged for personal gain is unacceptable in Machiavelli's system of heroic political ethics. He carefully distinguishes between cruelty used well or badly. As with Agathocles, the moral paradigm of ethics is held up as the criteria by which evil acts are evaluated despite any politically expedient goal they might serve. Glory for the prince will result only if he secures the common welfare.[29] It would be "sinful" to reject necessary evil out of qualms of conscience, or even worse, to do nothing at all.

Machiavelli's secular politicizing of sin suggests his attitude toward the function of religion in the state.[30] Ferdinand of Spain exemplifies the ruler who ". . . continually availed himself of religion . . . ," who in fact justified military aggression under the cloak of religion (ch. 21). Machiavelli's concern here is not to deemphasize the metaphysical implications of religion or the spiritual necessity of religion in saving men's souls, but rather to stress the often ignored social and political role of religion, Christian or pagan, in preserving the *virtù* of the state and in unifying the people for action beneficial to all. The fulfillment of one's political responsibilities is considered a religious duty, while their neglect is sinful.[31] Yet Machiavelli suggests that the practice of the Christian ideals of mercy, charity, forgiveness, etc., leads to political ineffectiveness if not total impotence. In the *Discourses,* 11 he specifies more explicitly than in *The Prince* how a Christian education in the contemplative virtues of monastic life fostered political idleness masking as saintly contempt for the things of this world. This is seen in *The Prince* when he exalts the men of action who undertook to shape their own destinies and those of the societies they led. For the theological virtues he substitutes the kind of civic devotion and involvement which characterized the heroes of the classical world. Machiavelli's criticism of Christianity is not, however, generalized or categorical, but rather intended to point out that only one side of the Christian religion has been emphasized, while the other, the more active and militant side, has been ignored.

Machiavelli's discussion in *The Prince*, 11 of ecclesiastical princedoms demonstrates his attitude toward the Church of Rome and how the papacy had affected the course of Italian politics. Again, the *Discourses* presents a more elaborate statement on this subject, but *The Prince* previews Machiavelli's belief that the Roman Church was in essence responsible for Italy's political failure. His memorable reply to Cardinal Rouen epitomizes Machiavelli's view of the Church's decisive role in European politics as well.[32] Ch. 11 begins by pointing out how ". . . customs grown old in church history . . ." have succeeded in preserving the temporal power of the pope, who despite political, administrative, and military inactivity, maintains security and prosperity for his states. His reference to the "superior causes" assuring this success surfaces the ironic and at times sarcastic tone typical of Machiavelli's style.[33] Machiavelli implies that people fear to rebel against the pope's temporal authority because in these states religion has been so institutionalized as to become identical with the state. In ecclesiastical princedoms the full power of religion as a politically authenticating instrument is evident. Although the temporal power of the Church existed for some time in Italy, it was only with Alexander VI that it solidified around the idea of freeing Italy of foreign domination. The chapter briefly surveys the weakness of the Church before Alexander VI, who ". . . using as his instrument Duke Valentino and as his opportunity the French invasion . . ." achieved unprecedented power. Julius II audaciously carried on ". . . to exalt the Church . . . ," while to Pope Leo X (Giovanni de' Medici), who ascended the papal throne March 11, 1513, Machiavelli offers his "best wishes" in achieving the same end.

Yet in the *Discourses* Machiavelli specifies that the Papacy should not become involved in Italian secular politics. Although religion as *instrumentum regni* provided strong political and social cohesion especially under emergency conditions, the application of effective politics in many situations was incompatible with Christian principles. Political leaders who also represented religious models would weaken religion and undermine internal stability. The corruption of the higher clergy and indeed of the Pope himself, as recent Italian history demonstrated, would fatally undercut both religion and politics. Machiavelli saw that in fact the Church had contributed to Italian divisiveness, since although it was powerful, it was insufficiently powerful to unite Italy herself, while preventing potential unifiers from achieving it as well.[34]

Few if any religious leaders functioned simultaneously as effective political leaders—as armed prophets such as Moses, who forced the continued observance of his institutions. Savonarola had failed because ". . . he had no way to keep firm those who had once believed or to make the unbelieving believe."[35] Yet even in Machiavelli's description of Moses (ch. 6) the same irony[36] pervades as in his description of the ecclesiastical princedoms. In fact, the two sections can be compared for their identity of idea and style. As in ch. 11 Machiavelli first disavows the appropriateness of discussing such an elevated subject, and then goes on indeed to make the very point he initially intended.[37] Moses is portrayed strictly as an astute, calculating political leader conscious of the powerful effect that religion can have in unifying a people against political crisis. Moses' supposed privileged status with God which made him the transmitter of God's commandments—a supposition Machiavelli asserts as fact—is viewed not as a religious milestone in human history, but rather as a deliberate political maneuver.[38] Moses exemplifies the new prince who acquired his princedom through his own masterly ability, through the advantageous exploitation of occasion and necessity, and through the adroit manipulation of the people's religious fears and sentiments. He epitomizes Machiavelli's ironic if not sarcastic assertion (ch. 26) that "God does not do everything, so as not to take from us free will and part of the glory that pertains to us." Machiavelli's audience might have been reminded of the often-repeated motto attributed to Cosimo de' Medici: "States are not maintained by reciting the rosary or the Lord's Prayer." In fact, they are not, but Moses, Cosimo, and Machiavelli understood that the effective ruler must *appear* to be praying, when in actuality he may be planning his political strategy.

## The Style of *The Prince*

The study of Machiavelli's literary and rhetorical style in *The Prince* has not received as much attention as that of his political concepts, yet the work that has been done reveals him to have had a literary consciousness as acute and as penetrating as his political awareness. A careful evaluation of his literary devices in *The Prince* links him in interesting ways both to Renaissance conventions and to the contemporary writers, English as well as continental. Whether Machiavelli wrote out of a desire to gain a political appointment, out of a need for self-therapy, or out of the inscrutable compulsions which motivate any artist, his work projects a self-consciousness and unique ability to synthesize the traditional with the innovative not unlike that of other great European writers of the time. Francis Bacon, Robert Burton, and Montaigne, like Machiavelli, demonstrate the remarkable genius to incorporate and subsume personal experience with more "scientific" interests into literary forms which have perennially fascinated subsequent generations. Although Machiavelli's style differs clearly from that before him in the history of Italian literature as to inspire some critics to call him the founder of modern Italian prose,[39] nevertheless, any analysis of Machiavelli's literary technique must be based on a comprehensive knowledge of Renaissance aesthetic and rhetorical theories and practices. Whereas today pronounced distinctions often exist between the media of prose and poetry, such distinctions did not exist in his time. Sir Philip Sidney, in his *An Apology for Poetry,* asserted that it was not rhyming that made poetry but rather the feigning of notable images of virtue and vice. Sidney defines "Poesy" as the art of imitation, or *mimesis,* a representing, counterfeiting, or figuring forth, a speaking picture intended to teach and delight. The prevalence of the aesthetic and rhetorical principles Sidney so brilliantly projects in his *Apology* authenticates the study of *The Prince* as a work of art, as indeed a "poem." It is interesting that Sidney, like Machiavelli, also cites Cyrus as a political, as well as an aesthetic, symbol and model for imitation.[40]

Machiavelli's prose has been praised for its emancipation from artifice, for its robust yet subtle use of language, and for its blending of logical and imaginative forms. His dramatic yet calculated use of hyperbole or understatement and his comfortable juxtaposition of erudite Latinisms with the colloquialisms of the Tuscan dialect convey an unparalleled and often shocking dynamism. DeSanctis said his prose ". . . is clear and rounded like a piece of marble, but marble with veins in it."[41] The "veins" often are in the form of the particular ways in which Machiavelli utilizes words in certain contexts. Critics have noted the importance of usage and context in understanding his meaning.[42] Hexter has analyzed Machiavelli's use of "value-bearing modifiers," such as good-well, bad-ill, within the "fabric of political imperatives of Machiavelli's own day," in an attempt to understand the effect of *The Prince*. He concludes that Machiavelli's use of specific words was not in their traditional Renaissance sense, but with altered connotations, suggesting that he perceived a disjunction "between the fabric of political imperatives and the conditions of effective political action."[43] Word usage combines with grammatical forms, parts of speech, and syntactic structures to intensify the dramatic effect of his prose.[44]

Machiavelli's achievement in the evolution of Italian prose must be seen within the background of the relationship between the humanistic aesthetic and the process of political change occurring in Italy from the fifteenth to the middle of the sixteenth century.[45] Even though his realistic politics based on experience and on the hypothetical analysis of political events seems to oppose the mainstream of the more idealistic and impractical humanist tradition, he nonetheless reflects the typical humanist concern for the dependence of politics on rhetoric to assist in achieving its civic goals. Machiavelli rejected the pompous eloquence of the idealistic humanists, but he did not reject the importance of rhetoric in the pursuit of a political idea.[46] He demonstrates how the realism of his political consciousness merged with the more literary and theoretical concerns of the rhetorical humanists. He employs style to convey his maxims with the hope of effecting political change. Thus, as for the humanists, rhetoric—the effective means of conveying truth—has an educational, cultural, and moral function.[47] Machiavelli's practical political goals relate to the concerns of achieving good government and good citizens which was characteristic of the pragmatic and civic oriented Florentine humanists. His use of literary devices is consistent with the humanist stylistic techniques. In their arguments based on example and authority they attempted, through verisimilitude, vividness and variety, to represent general types or to project universal lessons through concrete and emotionally convincing images, symbols, and other devices intended to persuade and stimulate the will.[48]

Machiavelli's use of imaginative devices such as concrete images conforms to the rhetorical and persuasive intentions behind the humanist aesthetic. The images or metaphors are for the most part drawn from the ordinary world which would have been well understood by his audience and thus increase their persuasive effect. Analogies, drawn from the vacillations of the weather, as in chs. 7, 9, and 24, present the subject, usually the prince or the state, as a natural object susceptible to the forces of nature. Images of the flooding river (chs. 25, 26) and of growing plants (ch. 7) heighten the naturalistic or scientific effect. These are supplemented by images of construction, building, or architecture (ch. 7) and those often-mentioned allusions drawn from medicine (chs. 3, 13), adding a dimension of organic growth and decay, health and disease, building and destroying to Machiavelli's political concepts. Whereas Machiavelli does in fact reject pompous ornamentation and amplifications, the nature of the rhetorical images he selects for their convincing effect preserves the scientific, factual, or technical quality of his discussion.[49]

Although a surface quality of factualism interpreted by moderns as a "scientific" tone pervades *The Prince,* in Machiavelli's time the modern distinctions between art and science did not prevail. Other seemingly scientific devices, such as the method of division and subdivision (ch. 1, 3, 4, 5, 8), whereby he distinguishes types of princedoms, or lists Louis's six mistakes, or analyzes the two types of state, or specifies two ways of rising from private station, or categorizes three kinds of intelligence, etc., appear together with more imaginative devices such as allegorical figuration and biblical allusion. Examples from experience or authority appear with psychological analysis of motives and their effects (ch. 6). Run-of-the-mill summaries or histories of mercenaries (ch. 12) or of popes (ch. 11) appear with persuasive and dramatic hypothesized dialogue (ch. 16). Incisive proverbs and epigrammatic assertions, assuming often the air of religious verity, are juxtaposed with subjective, often ironic or sarcastic polemical argumentation expressed in elaborate, repetitive, parallel sentence structure (ch. 16). This synthesis of science with art, of the common with the distant, of the popular with the erudite, of the theoretical with the concrete accounts for the dialectical dynamism of Machiavelli's style. It is primarily this quality of sustained artistic synthesis of diverse stylistic and conceptual elements which protects *The Prince* against accusations of fragmentation and structural disunity. The political, historical, and literary, the classical and popular, the scientific (factual) and the imaginative are fused by the clarity and organization of Machiavelli's all-encompassing humanistic perspective to produce a work with resoundingly original, if not lyrical, dimensions. His political intelligence and vocation are fused with his literary skills and poetical fantasy to epitomize one of the finest examples of the Renaissance amalgamation of art, politics, and history.

Just as *The Prince,* 1 announces the scope of the subject to be discussed, the final chapter summarizes Machiavelli's conceptual focus, stylistic methods, and artistic force. It exemplifies the progressive and retrogressive motion of his proposed method described at the beginning of ch. 2 when he promised to proceed ". . . by weaving [*tessendo*] together the threads mentioned . . ." in ch. 1. Ch. 26 subsumes the various threads of his argument: the focus on the new prince, his aspirations of glory for himself and happiness for the polis, the necessity of prudence and *virtù* in the leader, the significance of occasion, necessity, and *fortuna* in the outcome of events, the advantages of the ecclesiastical princedom and of the religiously inspired leader and people over the less stable, less motivated civil princedom, and the importance of skillful military leaders and a trained army. The obvious tone of exhortation characterizing the chapter, and leading some critics to conclude wrongly that it is disconnected from the rest of the work,[50] coincides with the humanist oratorical practice of arousing the audience, in this case the work's addressee, to apply the precepts of effective political action. The sentence structure in the first paragraph which repeats the allusions made earlier in ch. 6 to Moses, Cyrus, Romulus, and Theseus—its excitingly accelerated rhythm, its parallelism, repetitive syntax, and hyperbole—contributes to a heightened effect of exhortative appeal which seems to set the chapter apart from the rest of *The Prince*. Yet other aspects link it closely to the whole. It continues the practice of citing past history (the quote from Livy, *History*, 9.1.10). The imagery is the same as that used in earlier chapters; for example, the river-flood and medical allusions. The medical images are intensified from the references to fever and disease in previous chapters to metaphors in this chapter dealing with wounds festering (". . . heal her [state] wounds . . . ," "cure her of those sores already . . . festered"). The continuity is furthered also by the technical description, consistent with sections in the rest of *The Prince*, of the Swiss and Spanish infantry, French cavalry, and German battalions. Machiavelli, as he does throughout *The Prince*, skillfully blends this technical military description with the more poetical qualities and heroic tone for which ch. 26 has been so often noted. The new prince is transformed into a spiritual redeemer,[51] whose role transcends that of mere civic leadership to assume the messianic dimensions of Moses' rule over the Hebrews. The thematic implications of Machiavelli's major images—medicine, flooding, etc.—are subsumed into a single powerful theme, that of communal regeneration, or the cleansing of the polis. With this regeneration and reanimation of political fervor he associates miraculous natural phenomena described in apocalyptic language. The Medici, and specifically Giuliano, are portrayed as ordained by God to lead Italy's redemption. The event is marked, Machiavelli says, by ". . . unexampled signs that God is directing you: the sea is divided; a cloud shows you the road; the rock pours out water; manna rains down . . ."—singular and extraordinary happenings occurring during the Hebrews' march led by Moses toward the promised land (Exodus 14:17).

Undoubtedly, ch. 26 is one of the most remarkable examples of Renaissance literary art inspired by political motives. It merges the qualities of ease and familiarity, typical of the epistolary style found later in Montaigne's essays, with the uplifting and visionary elements of prophetic poetry. The correspondence of the Italian and Florentine situation with that of the Jews in a long distant past contributes to the sense of the timelessness of the problem, to humanity's tireless search for truth and justice, to the universality and continuity of historical events and human nature. Ch. 26 of *The Prince*, whether an afterthought or not, epitomizes the rarefied culmination of Machiavelli's political insight, historical consciousness, and literary genius.

## Chapter Three
# The Art of the *Discourses*

Machiavelli's reputation has rested for the most part on *The Prince*—an unfortunate fact which ignores the relationship among his works and underestimates the quality and depth of his political, historical, and literary achievement. It is understandable that *The Prince* should attract such critical attention, since its brevity and compactness invite scrutiny. Yet it represents only a summary of topics developed more extensively in his other writings and particularly in the *Discourses on the First Decade of Titus Livius*. The *Discourses* is even more impressive than *The Prince* for the brilliance of its prose, for the subtlety of the ironic humor, for the breadth and depth of historical knowledge, for the psychological insight, and for the skillful, calculated use of logic, *exempla,* and analogy. It epitomizes Machiavelli's admiration for republican Rome and it demonstrates his continued search for practical, although not immediate, solutions to contemporary political problems based on his experience and on an imitation of successful past methods. The didacticism and exhortation of the twenty-sixth chapter of *The Prince* are intensified in the *Discourses* to the level of identifying rhetorical characteristics. Machiavelli's concern for stability and for the preservation of the state are again reinforced, but through a reverberating and concentrated dramatization of the intimate relationships among the concepts of *virtù, fortuna,* and *necessità.*

### The Relationship between *The Prince* and the *Discourses*

A surface evaluation of *The Prince* and the *Discourses* could lead to a questioning of Machiavelli's motives for writing each work. Since *The Prince* seems to advocate rule by one, while the *Discourses*

advances a republican theory, could Machiavelli have authored both
these works and still have been sincerely committed to the political
views expressed therein?[1] Significant areas of overlapping and similarity do exist between the two works, as, for example, in the topics
of mercenary and auxiliary troops (*P.* 12 and 13; *D.* II, 20), whether
it is better to be loved or feared (*P.* 17; *D.* III, 19–23), the im-
possibility of keeping faith under all conditions (*P.* 18; *D.* III,
40–2), and the futility of fortresses (*P.* 20; *D.* II, 24), among others.
Both works are based on an acute knowledge of human psychology
and on the necessity for acting according to what is and not what
ought to be. The public direction of Machiavelli's intention and
method in both works is to present a vision of the state as strong,
stable, united, effective, and morally regenerated.

The relationships between the two works are complicated not
only by whatever similarities and/or differences exist, but also by
the proximity, if not concomitance, of their composition. The exact
details of the chronology are by no means fixed, and critics have
advanced several theories based both on internal and external evidence. The traditional view is that by the summer of 1513, the year
of Machiavelli's removal from office, part of the *Discourses,* probably
Book I, was composed. He then began, or may have been simultaneously working on, *The Prince,* completing it by December of
that year. It is believed that during 1514–16 he worked on the
*Discourses,* while in 1516 he revised *The Prince.* Since all the historical
references in the *Discourses* do not extend beyond 1517, it is assumed
that by 1519 at the latest he completed work on the third book,
and began to write *The Art of War.*[2] This view is based mainly on
the statement appearing at the beginning of *The Prince,* 2 which
refers supposedly to the *Discourses* as though completed or certainly
well on the road to completion.[3] The view is reinforced by the fact
that the three references to *The Prince* in the *Discourses* appear in
Books II and III (II, 1.6; III, 19.2; III, 42.2), composed after *The
Prince.* Machiavelli's December 10, 1513, letter to Vettori affirms
the completion of *The Prince,* but manuscript evidence combined
with the question of the change in the work's addressee suggest that
revisions occurred up to and during 1516.[4]

The differences between *The Prince* and the *Discourses* strongly outweigh any similarities. One difference is immediately evident in the rhetorical situations dramatized in the dedicatory epistles of the two works. *The Prince* is dedicated to one man, an actual ruler, while the *Discourses* is dedicated to two citizens, Zanobi Buondelmonti and Cosimo Rucellai, who, according to Machiavelli, although not princes themselves, ". . . on account of their innumerable good qualities, deserve to be. . . ."[5] Buondelmonti and Rucellai were members of the Orti Oricellari group which Machiavelli frequented a few years after his removal from office. Although there is no verification that Machiavelli read parts of his *Discourses* to meetings of this group, some of whose members favored republican government for Florence, it is likely that it discussed many of the topics found in the *Discourses* and that Machiavelli, as stated in the dedication, may have written it at their insistence.

While *The Prince* is concerned exclusively with principalities analyzed from the limited viewpoint of the prince, the *Discourses* surveys all forms of government, but primarily republics. *The Prince* considers how a sovereign obtains the state by hereditary right or by conquest. The ideal state here is epitomized in the *virtù* of the individual whose functions as the head of state are anatomized. Force and violence are valid, indeed necessary, means in the creation or restoration of a state. The political militancy and pragmatic tone emphasize the unrestricted authority of the prince as a founder of new states or as an initiator of regenerated modes and orders. As the founder of a society he possesses the requisite knowledge and exercises the privileges of power in establishing the state during this preliminary phase of its development. The primary historical figures who objectify this leader, Moses and Borgia, for example, symbolize the singleminded dedication and ruthlessness of the will-driven leader.

In analyzing the normal formation and complex evolution of the state, the *Discourses* specifies an ideal political organization based on the efficacious rule of law and justice. Rather than focusing on the *virtù* of the single leader, the *Discourses* stresses the *virtù* of a people who administer good laws and preserve ennobling customs and traditions, and as such the work has a wider applicability than *The*

*Prince*. By dedicating the *Discourses* to citizens who deserve to be princes but are not, Machiavelli presents the people as the sustainers of proven republican modes and orders and as the repository of morality and religion. In a critical and ethical tone Machiavelli's intention is to educate his audience on the structure of that society which will result in substantial political freedom and in an enduring civilization. The Roman republic demonstrated how a state is preserved—how it in fact operates as a living organism. The heroes here are lawgivers such as Romulus, Lycurgus, and Solon, among others, men who assumed power temporarily in order to establish laws for the common good, and then voluntarily relinquished their authority.

In attempting to reconcile these obvious differences between the two works, some critics view them as two parts of a single treatise on politics[6] or as not opposed because *The Prince* was supposedly not written with Florence specifically in mind.[7] Others defend the view of the discrete nature of the works,[8] consider the *Discourses* as a distinct intellectual advance in Machiavelli's political thought,[9] or see it as representing a different moment in the author's political experience—another phase of his passion for political technique.[10] The approach which perhaps does least justice to the relationship between *The Prince* and the *Discourses* is one which portrays Machiavelli as either an advocate of monarchical, if not tyrannical rule, or as an advocate of republicanism. Since Machiavelli was not an abstract political theorist, but rather concerned with actual political problems and the workable solutions which might best resolve them, he cannot be categorized so absolutely as preferring one or the other. His preference, as demonstrated by a close reading of both works, is governed by the historical context and political circumstances; in one instance strong rule by one man is required, in another, the people are seen to have the best judgment. Yet the overall impression one derives, especially after reading the *Discourses* in connection with *The Prince,* is that Machiavelli admires the political structure of republican Rome at its peak and wherever possible advises its emulation. The relationship between these two works cannot be simplistically characterized as one of despotism versus liberty, especially when these terms are so colored by our modern connotations. The concept of liberty for Machiavelli and his age did not mean individual, ethical freedom to do and think as one pleases, but rather it is closely associated with necessity and law. Laws are the artificial substitute for necessity and as such protect the *vivere libero* ("the free life") of a state. Laws impose limits and restrictions which insure the common interest over individual selfish desires. Laws function like necessity, inspiring men to actions worthy of not just fame, but glory.[11]

The supposed dichotomy between *The Prince* and the *Discourses* is also projected in the heroic figures Machiavelli employs to exemplify his ideas in the two works. Obviously, the figure of the prince as a political redeemer dominates the former work, while the image of the lawgiver as founder or restorer dominates the latter. Yet there is an undeniable relationship between the prince and the legislator and the function of reformer which both may have to assume at some point. The *virtù* of the single, self-willed organizer determines the actual birth of a new republic or a kingdom, or their renewal after a period of decadence.[12] It was the *virtù* of Aeneas and Romulus in Rome, Lycurgus in Sparta, Theseus and Solon in Athens—the prudence and foresight they demonstrated in originating political and civil laws and institutions—which was responsible for these great societies. The lawgiver operates as a prince for a time, but once the political institutions are established, if he is wise and disinterested, he withdraws his princely power but continues to infuse a spirit of cohesion and strength as the institutions operate at the direction of the people.

Although the *Discourses* was not published until 1531 by Blado in Rome, four years after Machiavelli's death, the work was available in manuscript form before then.[13] The two works did not provoke, during Machiavelli's lifetime or even for sometime thereafter, the concern about their apparent dualisms and contradictions and it would seem that this problem originated with modern scholarship. The Renaissance was much more attuned to works rhetorically inspired with a particular audience in mind and much less concerned with the clearcut, specialized distinctions typical of our approach to philosophical issues. The question of the relationships between *The Prince* and *Discourses* simply represents one aspect of the general question of the interrelationship among all of Machiavelli's writings. *The Art of War*, begun while Machiavelli was still working on the Discourses, reveals much of the same topic overlapping discussed earlier, as does *The History of Florence*.[14]

## Dedication and Prefaces

As with the dedication of *The Prince*, the dedicatory epistle of the *Discourses* claims that the work expresses the author's complete knowledge of political affairs based on his long experience and on his reading of history. He categorizes the work as a gift to his two close friends, Zanobi Buondelmonti and Cosimo Rucellai, to whom he is obliged, and who apparently had forced him to write it. After acknowledging his lack of skill and errors of judgment, he explains that he has departed from the usual practice of authors who, blinded by ambition and avarice, dedicate their works to princes who may have the right to govern but not the knowledge or ability. He has chosen to dedicate his *narrazioni*, the *Discourses*, to his citizen-friends, not only because of his gratitude for benefits received, but because they, like Hiero of Syracuse (271–216 B.C.), possess all of the qualities to be princes in their own right. The rhetorical intention of this dedication highlights the role of the private citizen in the state and his potential to participate wisely in its government despite his lack of princely power. The inherent value and necessity for princely power is, in fact, minimized by his assertion that qualifications, such as historical knowledge, and *virtù*, not power, should be the determining factors in selecting a ruler. Machiavelli may have been thinking of his own exclusion from governmental service, despite his years of experience and obvious qualifications. In any case, the emphasis is placed on the kind of political situation, namely a republic, where the role and voice of the private citizen would be crucial.

While the dedication stresses the theme of republicanism, the preface to Book I announces and defines his new methodological approach—". . . to discover new ways and methods . . ." and thus ". . . enter upon a new way, as yet untrodden by anyone else." His main purpose in this preface is to point out that while in the arts, law, and medicine men turn to history for models, precedents, and cures that will bring a new life to their art, in politics such knowledge is admired rather than imitated and often even shunned. Although Machiavelli attributes this neglect of the past ". . . to people failing to realise the significance of what they read, and to their having no taste for the delicacies it comprises . . . ," he suggests through negation that in fact it is ". . . the weak state to which the religion of today has brought the world, or to the evil wrought in many provinces and cities of Christendom by ambition conjoined with idleness . . ." that is responsible for this condition. This deplorable state, combined with the encouragement received from his friends, has led him to attempt to restore the lost *virtù* of antiquity by educating men on the need for both the prince and the republic to turn to ancient times for examples. By writing a commentary on the extant books of Livy which compares ancient with modern events, he hopes to prove that there is a pattern in history, that the laws of cause and effect govern politics in the same ways they govern inanimate nature, and thus produce a work which will ". . . get men out of this wrong way of thinking . . . ," correct the political disorder of his time, and thus have ". . . common benefit for all."[15]

The preface to Book II, twice as long as that to Book I, continues the theme of the relationship of the past to the present, but Machiavelli employs a more subtle rhetorical device to justify his methodological approach of elevating the authority of the past. He begins by seeming critical of the intrusion of nostalgia to distort men's judgment of the past and especially of their youth. Machiavelli admits how the obsequiousness of writers to the fortune of conquerors, how exaggeration and magnification contribute to the error of an unscrutinizing evaluation of the past. Yet he explains that this is understandable since men neither fear nor envy the past. Subtly shifting his tone, he says that although those living in a state at a time when it is steadily improving certainly have little cause to praise the past over the present, such an opinion would be valid for those who were not so fortunate. Change and decline are inescapable factors in any civilization, leading Machiavelli to assert his theory of the evolution of *virtù* from state to state—first appearing in Assyria, then flourishing in Media, Persia, Italy, and Rome consecutively. Since the fall of Rome no country has possessed *virtù* with its intensity and durability, even though certain ones, such as France, Turkey, and Germany, have shared in it to some extent. *Virtù* is so lacking in present day Italy that Machiavelli believes himself justified in looking to the past for virtuous models to contrast with the vices obvious in contemporary princes and legislators. Repeating the didactic theme of the earlier preface, Machiavelli explains that his purpose is to educate the minds of young men on admirable models, since ". . . it is the duty of a good man to point out to others what is well done, even though the malignity of the times or of fortune has not permitted you to do it for yourself, to the end that, of the many who have the capacity, someone, more beloved of heaven, may be able to do it."[16]

The dedication and the prefaces are important for the statements Machiavelli makes on his purpose and method in the *Discourses* and perhaps more for what they reveal about his rhetorical strategies and their relationship to the content of the work.[17]

## Machiavelli's Sources, "New Method," and Structure

The *Discourses,* more than any of Machiavelli's works, exemplifies his unique approach and contribution to political writing of clarifying and codifying effective past principles. As he points out in the prefaces, art, law, and medicine had for years applied the knowledge gained from a study of classical sources, and in asserting a new method—the systematizing of historical lessons—Machiavelli was doing for politics what had already been done for the other disciplines. The *Discourses* were intended as a traditional literary commentary on perhaps the best of the Roman sources on politics and history. As a commentary, and not a chronological paraphrase, it analyzes selected topics, historical events, and figures found in Livy with the intention of extending their significance to the contemporary Florentine scene. Machiavelli did not restrict himself to Livy, including as well many references to Polybius' *History*, Cicero's *Republic*, Aristotle's *Politics*, Plato's *Republic* and *Laws*, among other authors.[18]

Machiavelli's method is based on the idea of the remedial return to a state's origins. Experience of present affairs combined with a thoughtful evaluation of the past encourage such an idea. Yet Machiavelli does not simply advise an indiscriminate modern imitation of classical antiquity; rather he sets out to present *modi et ordini nuovi,* what Strauss has called ". . . new political 'arrangements' in regard to both structures and policies."[19] Therefore, Machiavelli's concern was not simply to discover a new method of studying history and politics, but of actually suggesting practices and institutions which had proven successful in ancient times but for centuries had been so neglected that they now could be considered new. His concern is motivated by a pragmatic intention to correct contemporary mistakes and to serve the common good. In outlining his argumentative approach in the *Discourses,* we can determine three major techniques, employed not always sequentially: (1) inductive and/or deductive organization of the discussion; (2) a critical, analytical, and comparative study of the past and the present using examples and experience to clarify general principles; (3) admonishment and exhortation to change current practices and imitate the past.

As the basis of his discussion Machiavelli used Livy's first ten books of the *History of Rome (Ab urbe condita libri),* covering the years 753 B.C. to 293 B.C., when Rome's constitution, political institutions, military organization, and empire were evolving. Yet he did not systematically restrict himself by the source's chronology. Rather, he disguised the conventional aspect of the work by avoiding an absolute exegetic commentary and by developing his own structure founded on a combination of temporal and thematic concerns.[20] He divided the *Discourses* into the traditional tripartite division, each book dealing selectively with many of the same events of Rome's history covered by Livy, but presenting a different major theme and point of view. Book I treats Rome's internal affairs from the perspective of constitutional changes, new institutions and laws enacted by the people. Book II deals with Rome's foreign affairs, especially waging war, conquests, and alliances, transacted on the basis of public counsel, whose effect was to increase the geographic span of the empire. Book III analyzes what was done on the initiative of Rome's eminent private citizens to make Rome a great and enduring power.[21]

## *Virtù, Fortuna,* and *Necessità* in the *Discourses*

The major point which distinguishes Machiavelli's treatment of these concepts in the *Discourses* from that in *The Prince* is that in the latter work his observations are directed toward an individual who would be the leader of the state at a particular historical moment, while in the *Discourses* his observations encompass the individual but extend beyond to the citizens who comprise the state and whose *virtù* is evidenced over a long period of time in the legal, educational, and religious institutions. *Discourses,* I, 19 contains about ten occurrences of the word *virtù* and can be considered a crucial chapter in determining Machiavelli's meaning of the word in this work.[22] *D.* I, 19, "A Weak Prince who succeeds an Outstanding Prince can hold his own, but a Weak Prince who succeeds another Weak Prince cannot hold any Kingdom," discusses three sets of successive rulers each demonstrating that a succession of strong kings can result in a nation's greatness, while a succession of weak kings brings inevitable ruin. The emblematic evocation of figures and episodes from the common denominator of Roman history provides the most convincing evidence. Romulus, fierce and warlike in disposition, was followed by Numa, peaceful and religious, who in turn was succeeded by Tullus, a lover of war and devoted to the soldierly arts. This succession of kings, who possessed the necessary set of qualities at a particular stage in Rome's historical evolution, helped to establish its military strength and political permanence. The same point is made by the examples of David, Solomon, and Rehoboam in biblical history, and Mahomet, Bajazet, and Selim in contemporary Turkish history. Thus, while Machiavelli here, as in *The Prince,* is discussing the *virtù* needed by princes to hold their dominions, his real focus is on succession and permanency, on how the *virtù* of successive leaders determines the progress and stability of a state, and on how the individual *virtù* of leaders will foster collective *virtù.* Such an analytical focus on succession and permanence and on the interrelationship of individual and collective *virtù* coincides with Machiavelli's emphasis in the *Discourses* on the evolution and perpetuation of republican *modi et ordini*. The qualities of individual *virtù*—courage, energy, civic dedication, strength of will, resourcefulness, prudence, etc.—are depersonalized and extended from the single leader, who achieves great deeds, to the collective body that must, as the Romans did, strive for political success through military discipline and bravery. Success in this context means the evolution of efficient and effective republican institutions and the preservation of republican freedom.

The opposition of *virtù* to *fortuna* which helps to delimit and define the nature and scope of each concept in *The Prince* also is found in the *Discourses*. Several chapters depict this dynamic interrelation of the politically calculable with the unexpected or unforeseen. In *D*. II, 1, "Whether Virtue or Fortune was the Principal Cause of the Empire which Rome acquired," Machiavelli debunks the view of the ancient historians, Plutarch and Livy, regarding the reasons for Rome's greatness. Machiavelli isolates three supporting arguments: (1) the Roman armies always showed great valor and the Roman people supported their army's efforts by never being forced to carry on two wars at the same time, and thus debilitate and disperse its power; (2) prudent constitutional procedures; and (3) a calculated foreign policy which permitted Rome to gain strong footholds abroad. Perhaps the most interesting aspect of this discussion is Machiavelli's disagreement with Livy and Plutarch who attributed Rome's greatness to fortune rather than *virtù*. In relating this aspect to Machiavelli's assertion that he will take a "new road" in his analysis of the relationship of history to the present, it demonstrates that his approach in the *Discourses* is far from an imitative confirmation of Livy, or any ancient historian. Rome's success lay in her conjoining of *virtù* and fortune, in the shrewdness with which she managed her wars, in her premeditated cultivation of enough power to intimidate if not completely deter her enemies from attack, and in her ability to lull her enemies into unreadiness.

*D*. III, 9, "That it behooves one to adapt Oneself to the Times if one wants to enjoy Continued Good Fortune," further explores the relationship of *virtù* to *fortuna*, but from the perspective of the example of Rome's great men, the main subject of Book III, rather than from the point of view of how Rome as a nation increased its empire through military conquest, as in Book II. Machiavelli explains why men are fortunate or unfortunate in terms of the adaptability of their behavior to what the times require. Man's behavior is dictated by his nature—an inborn set of traits, ways, and habits which he cannot change because first, it is impossible to go against nature, and second, man will recur indiscriminately to previously successful lines of conduct, even if the times are not appropriate for this kind of behavior. The times were conducive to the cautiousness of a Fabius, the impetuosity of a Scipio, the rashness of a Julius II, but Piero Soderini's goodnatured, patient manner was unsuited to the crisis in the Florentine republic in 1512. Yet Machiavelli's analysis of individual cases functions as analogous support for the generalized observations he incorporates into the chapter about republics. The examples of Fabius and Scipio lead to the conclusion that a republic will survive longer than a principality because it can call upon the diversity of its citizenry to deal with various circumstances. Soderini's downfall, and Julius II's potential for ruin, is compared to the downfall of republican cities where institutions fail to change with the times, ". . . but change very slowly because it is difficult to change them since it is necessary to wait until the whole republic is disposed to make the change; and for this it is not enough that one man alone should change his own procedure."[23]

The comparative analogy between men and republics is continued in *D*. III, 31, "Strong Republics and Outstanding Men retain their Equanimity and their Dignity under all Circumstances." The outstanding men in a republic, who objectify the *virtù* inherent in the republic itself, always are found to remain resolute and dignified in mind and conduct despite the vagaries of fortune. One must take care not to misuse good fortune in prosperous times by becoming arrogant, since such behavior renders you defenseless and could cause a sudden change in fortune. One must never become disheartened and dejected at defeat, however, since there is always hope. Camillus, an outstanding Roman, credited by Livy with saying, "The dictatorship did not elate me, nor did exile depress me," objectifies the resolute, composed manner with which the Roman republic responded to changes in fortune. The Romans, because of good laws and arms, courage, and preparation, were always superior to Fortune, in contrast to the contemporary example of the Venetians, who mistakenly judged their good fortune as due to a virtue which they did not in fact possess. A similarly extreme reaction typified their despondency at defeat, exposing their inflexible political institutions and weak military discipline. Just as a man's behavior in victory or defeat is determined by his background, his understanding of human nature and of the world, and his education, so too a republic's collective behavior is dictated by its civic and military institutions.

The designs and operations of fortune are mysterious and often unpredictable, as vividly explored in *D.* II, 29, "Fortune blinds Men's Minds when she does not wish them to obstruct her Designs." In explaining inscrutable fortune, Machiavelli offers insight into its relationship to individual *virtù* and to the fate of a whole people, and how both are often governed by necessity. Through the Livian example of Rome's almost catastrophic initial experience with the Gauls, Machiavelli in this instance confirms the Roman historian's maxim that man is defenseless before the willful designs of fortune who will arbitrarily choose certain men to promote failure or success. Rome's experience with the Gauls stresses the role of necessity in a nation's ultimate destiny, since it allowed Rome to be chastised, but not ruined, and it permitted her recovery and eventual triumph. The example thus shows that no matter how dire or extreme circumstances may seem, men and republics should never lose hope, for they are incapable of deciphering the labyrinthian ordinances of fortune.

## The Role of the People in the Political Psychology of the *Discourses*

The dedicatory epistle to *The Prince* presents an extended metaphor of the people occupying the plain and the prince ruling from the high mountain, a metaphor which subtly camouflages what Machiavelli believes to be his uniquely authoritative position in evaluating the difference of political vision between the prince or the aristocracy *(grandi)* on the one hand, and the common people on the other. Yet *The Prince* does not focus on explaining the people's perspective or on defining the nature of their role in the political life of a state. It is the behavior of the new prince on which Machiavelli focuses, and the people, while they are recognized as significant, are acknowledged only in terms of what the new prince must do in order to control and secure his dominance over them. In the *Discourses* Machiavelli explores the role of the people in the initiation, development, decay, and rebirth of a republican state. His concept of the people's role is dictated by the realistic psychological foundations of his attitude toward man. He believed that the innately aggressive, agonistic, and selfish natures of man must be controlled by a well-ordered and disciplined state if the common good is to prevail over individual self-interest. Man is driven by contradictory passions and inclinations: love-fear, courage-cowardice, need for tranquility—longing for adventure, among others. His ambition, suspicion, envy, insatiability, and general antisocial behavior confirm his essentially depraved nature, a depravity found constant in the history of man's actions. The persistence of man's depravity justifies the comparison of ancient and present man, for in both cases man's evil caused social upheaval and political disorder. His destructive competitiveness instigated divisions which are best mollified in the long run by a republican form of government advancing the collective interest of the state through proper leadership and active civic involvement by the people.[24] Machiavelli's concern with the role of the people in a republic is intended primarily to show how to prevent the rule of a founder, reformer, or new prince from developing into despotism and tyranny.

Although Machiavelli acknowledges that the people can often be disorderly, confused, and emotional, he recognizes as well that they are concerned with the preservation of political, social, and economic freedom, and that their passive or active behavior will cumulatively influence the performance of the rulers and the organic and historic life of the state. The rulers must respect the people and know how to lead, control, and organize them in such a way as to assure their continued goodwill and support. The rulers should realize that the people could threaten the stability and security of a state if they are unduly repressed and if appropriate public platforms and other outlets for popular discontent and ambition are not provided.[25] In *D.* I, 58, "The Masses are more Knowing and more Constant than is a Prince," Machiavelli shows that he does not slavishly follow or accept his source, by rejecting Livy's remark that "Nothing is more futile and more inconstant than are the masses." In a rhetorically argumentative stance, he defends the proposition that the nature of the populace is no more reprehensible than that of the prince, and that it is often more prudent, stable, and of sounder judgment. The prince may excel the masses in drawing up laws, civil codes, statutes, and new institutions, but the people are superior in preserving and nurturing what has been instituted, and more honest and less ungrateful than princes.

The dichotomy between prince or ruling class and the people results from two basic humors *(umori)* or natural dispositions. The *grandi* desire to have power and to command others, while the populace desires not to be repressed or mistreated (*D*. I, 4). Machiavelli recognizes man's innate inclination to create factions (see *D*. I, 4, 18, 5, 60; III, 16, 25, 19) which, in their attempt to acquire political ascendancy through the use of any method from the legal vote to murder, could be dangerous and possibly even destructive to the life of the state. Florentine history demonstrated what would occur if one faction usurped rights denied to others and if that faction resorted to bribery, corruption, and homicide to assure that the government would adopt its policies. Yet in *D*. I, 4 Machiavelli shows how humoric struggle (also see *The Prince,* 9)—the conflicting human appetites which originate either a principality or republic on the one hand, or license and anarchy on the other—in the Roman republic was contained and directed by skillful political leadership. The Romans exemplify how divisions in human nature were managed by the creation of political outlets and institutions which assured that each group had adequate political representation and influence. The Romans did not avoid humoric struggle, but successfully circumvented the potentially destructive effects of unmanaged political and social hostilities between rival groups in a state. In fact, Machiavelli judges that the Romans were so effective at understanding and controlling the innate psychological *umori* behind political behavior that the discord between the nobles and the plebes was the primary cause of her retaining her freedom. The clash between the upper class and the populace resulted in legislation which ultimately insured a free and powerful state. The analysis of how Rome dealt with political and social dissension resulting from factional and class divisions especially during the early phase of its republican history operates as a dominant theme in *D. I*. Machiavelli shows that the obvious tumultuousness of Roman history was used constructively and creatively to mold a great and glorious state.[26]

## The Operative Function of Religion

In *D. I*, 11–15 Machiavelli demonstrates explicitly the point made in *The Prince* that religion is an important political instrument and its skillful use or imprudent neglect will determine the success of any ruler or state. In *The Prince,* religion is ironically a device of fraudulent self-recommendation and self-concealment for the new prince, since one founding or regenerating a state can neither reveal to the people his intentions to rule nor his true nature. Machiavelli does not deny the personal, charismatic function of religion, but in the *Discourses* he is concerned with specifying its secular function, civic, political, and military. The history of the rulers who succeeded Romulus shows the importance of religion in promoting and sustaining civic institutions and laws. While Romulus' fierce, warlike nature was appropriately conducive to the establishment of a new state, his successor, Numa, preserved and extended Romulus' achievement by using religion rather than war. As the founder of the Roman religion, Numa appealed to the people's superstitions and fears in introducing new civic and military institutions to which the city was unaccustomed (*D. I*, 11). Realizing that his own authority might not suffice in his wish to reduce the people to civic obedience and discipline, Numa pretended to have private conferences with a divine nymph and, thus, gained divine authority for the extraordinary laws needed to maintain a civilized state. Throughout Roman history religion operated as a unifying, cohesive force, controlling armies, encouraging the plebs, nurturing good men, and shaming the bad; it inspired good laws, promoted the common good, facilitated propitious, fortune and continued political and military success.[27] In *D. I*, 13 Machiavelli exemplifies how the Romans used religion to reform their city and to carry on their wars. Roman generals, such as Camillus, resorted to pretense—the assigning of religious interpretations to pestilences and famine—to keep the troops controlled and keyed up for battle, as exemplified by the Roman siege of Veii. *D.* I, 14 shows through the positive example of Papirius how Roman generals astutely and prudently accommodated and contravened auguries and auspices, the basis of the Roman religion, to their military plans. The adroitness with which they twisted the customary divination by poultry so that they did not appear to have done anything disparaging to religion caused the troops to enter battle with the confidence which assured military *virtù* and success.

The Christian states had neglected the principles of Christianity's founder and had failed to imitate Rome's example of using religion, particularly its rites, ceremonies, and anthropomorphic beliefs, to buttress political institutions and ideologies. Despite the attempts of religious reformers such as St. Francis and St. Domenic to restore decadent Christianity to the principles of poverty and other virtues exemplified in the life of Christ (*D.* III, 1), the political policies of the Popes and the actions of the Church prelates had nullified the effect of its moral teaching and of any periodic renovations. Through its impiety and irreligiousness, the Church of Rome had impeded national unity and fostered a decline of military discipline. Seeing itself above the people rather than at the service of the people, as was the case with the paganism of ancient Rome, the Church promoted perverse division from within and barbaric invasion from without (*D.* I, 12). Moreover, although Machiavelli nowhere condemns the conventional values of Christian morality—humility, self-sacrifice, abnegation, contempt for the worldly, among others—he points out that such virtues encourage men to bear adversity in this life rather than to avenge their injuries. Such forbearance allows rule by the weak and the wicked, who realize that most men have paradise as their goal rather than the advancement of the social and political goals best for a nation (*D.* II, 2). Unlike in Christian times, in ancient Rome the religious ceremonies were observed with great attention, pomp, and magnificence (*D.* I, 12; II, 2). The barbaric, savage beauty of pagan sacrificial offerings, their bloodshedding and ferocity, inspired awe, fear, and devotion, and proved that the Romans respected the power of God, as communicated by the oracles, soothsayers, and diviners, more than the power of men. The differences between Christianity and paganism are the basis for the differences between ancient and contemporary education. Paganism held worldly honor, bodily strength, and boldness in high esteem; it inspired a love for liberty and it beatified heroic men of action who had achieved worldly glory and fame. Machiavelli attributes the existence of fewer republics in his time than in ancient times to the fact that Christianity was interpreted as sloth and men had forgotten that religion permits them to exalt and defend the fatherland. Since civilization had corrupted men so, he admits that even were one to use religion to serve political ends, it would be difficult to establish a republic (*D*. I, 11). Just as the sculptor would ". . . more easily carve a beautiful statue from rough marble than from marble already spoiled by a bungling workman . . . ," so would it be easier to establish a republic among uncultured, rude mountaineers than among civilized citydwellers, for it is much easier to persuade simple men to adopt new institutions or a new point of view. Yet the example of Savonarola proves that it is not impossible, since he persuaded the people of Florence, who considered themselves neither ignorant nor rude, that he had conversed with God. Therefore, while Machiavelli indicts the Papacy, Christian rulers, and erroneous, perverse interpretations of Christianity, he exalts the use of religion for political purposes in ancient Rome and advocates its emulation by contemporary rulers and states.

## Style in the *Discourses*

As in subject matter, the *Discourses* represents an extention and elaboration of many of the rhetorical and stylistic devices found in *The Prince*. The length of the *Discourses* and the limited space available for comment allow for only a few general observations on the particular quality of the style in this work. Machiavelli's literary method is one of dialectical, ironic, and indirect argumentation. In an unsystematized but dynamic way, he employs contradiction, association, exhortation, metaphor, and multiple, often antithetical, points of view to present his commentary on Livy.[28] The imaginative and rhetorical force behind his politicohistorical vision and structure in the *Discourses* is gaining greater recognition in the attempt to clarify the obscurities and explain the inconsistencies evidenced throughout the work.[29] The question of the sincerity and straightforwardness of Machiavelli's expression in the *Discourses* immediately arises to anyone who reads the work with care and sensitivity to language and particularly tone. Machiavelli's writings in general, and the *Discourses* specifically, display a skillful and deliberate use of subtle, and at times camouflaging, rhetorical devices. His frequent allusions to the use of fraud, for example, in *D.* I, 11, 13, and 14, where he discusses how religion may operate as an instrument of dissimulation, are tinged with an ironic and even humorous quality. Particularly revealed in *D.* I, 14, the incident of how Papirius manipulated the auspices taken by the poultrymen shows how Machiavelli's surface statements conceal multiple levels of meaning and ironically reveal the deceptive nature of appearance which manifests itself as reality. Bondanella has shown how Machiavelli uses irony in his portrayal of historical characters as *exempla,* as in *D.* I, 27, when Machiavelli describes Giampaolo Baglioni at Perugia using ironic diction bordering on sarcasm to reflect Machiavelli's contempt for the man. Again, in *D.* I, 40, Machiavelli's version of Appius Claudius differs from Livy's (Book 3, 38–58) in that by shifting the focus of the account away from the redemptive sacrifice of Appius' daughter, Virginia, to an analysis of his nature, Machiavelli demonstrates how his shrewd, hypocritical, and ambitious nature is revealed in his deeds.[30] Yet the use of rhetorical manipulation and fictional addition to historical incidents was not unique to Machiavelli. His conscious and deliberate use of fictitious, imaginary, and other rhetorical enhancement was also typical of Xenophon's *Education of Cyrus* and Livy's *Decades.*[31] The comparison of Machiavelli's literary method to that of the poet applies not only to his character portrayal and story development, but also to his metaphorical use of language in the *Discourses.* The ironic and dualistic effect of his language is promoted by his use of the "either-or" disjunctive sentence and his use of words whose precise meaning can be determined only by their contextual reference. Moreover, the enigmatic and intriguing quality of his statements, whereby the full and lucid articulation of his meaning is deliberately withheld, is advanced by his poetic use of analogies, metaphors, and imagery. The use of metaphor ranges from singular analogies drawn from the worlds of medicine, art, and natural science to clarify some generalization, to the dramatic recommendation to kill the sons of Brutus (*D*. III, 3), to the overriding use of Rome as an historical mirage which poetically deflects, foils, and cushions the contemporary relevance of Machiavelli's often shocking penetration of surface reality.[32]

## Chapter Four
# War, Politics, and Rhetoric

*De re militari* [The Art of War], recounting conversations held by the Orti Oricellari group sometime in 1516, was begun in 1518, completed in 1520, and published in Florence by Giunta in 1521 after Machiavelli had edited the manuscript. His discussion of the technical and strategic aspects of war extends ideas in *The Prince* and the *Discourses*. Critical misunderstanding of *The Art of War*, like that of *The Prince*, emerges from a failure (1) to place it in the proper historical context, (2) to relate it to Machiavelli's other writings, and (3) to assess the work's rhetorical and humanistic dimensions.

Charles VIII's 1494 invasion of Italy initiated a series of devastating battles and humiliating defeats which would render the previously independent Italian states victims of foreign domination and exploitation. The war-filled 1500s signaled a change from the relatively peaceful conditions on the peninsula in the 1400s, sustained primarily by Lorenzo the Magnificent's keen personal diplomacy. Italian life thrived during this period, unscathed by foreign invasion and expansionism. Many blamed her failure in confronting Charles's challenge on the previous neglect of military life in favor of cultural goals. Florence suffered from this neglect, as evidenced in its financially draining, morally exhausting, and militarily ineffective attempts to subdue Pisa. Machiavelli played a direct role in these efforts, gaining much of the military experience which would solidify his views. Italy's military crisis coupled with Florence's problems determined the purpose, scope, and solutions Machiavelli presented in *The Art of War*. Firsthand and vicarious experiences proved the incontrovertible dependency of political and military life. In his view military failure resulted from low civic morale, bad laws, lax discipline, and ineffectual political leaders. The vulnerable political situation had permitted the continuation of the *condottieri*-mercenary system of waging war. The reform advocated in *The Prince* and the *Discourses* would succeed only if buttressed by a strong citizen militia led by committed, loyal generals with a personal stake, other than monetary, in the outcome. Thus, political and military regeneration must go hand in hand, and it is this reforming motive which inspired *The Art of War* as it did Machiavelli's two previous works. Although he deals with technical military questions as they relate to historical problems, his approach has an important humanistic and rhetorical dimension. The didactic, reformative intention—to teach, persuade, and change men—is defined first, in the preface, reiterated throughout, and eloquently reaffirmed in the final pages. Reinforcing the work's humanistic overtones is the use of the traditional dialogue form with a particularized setting, a speaking voice seemingly disassociated from the author, apparently naive interlocutors, and fictionalized conversations. Yet it is in the adaptation of Greek and Roman military methods to the contemporary situation—the comprehensive solution to military failure—that the humanistic quality of this work is most evident.

*The Art of War* summarizes Machiavelli's ideas on the military anticipated in his earliest writings on the subject, such as in the *Discourse on How to Arm the State of Florence* and the *Discourse on the Ordinance and on the Florentine Militia*, both written in 1506.[1] *The Art of War* develops the central and final chapters of *The Prince* (12 to 14; 24 and 26), numerous chapters in the *Discourses*, as well as many passages in *The History of Florence*. Just as *The Prince* asserts the political autonomy of the principality founded on the *virtù* of its ruler, and the *Discourses* demonstrates the establishment of independence based on the Roman model of republicanism, *The Art of War* affirms military autonomy as an essential corollary to political sovereignty and liberty. While *The Prince* propounds a new mode of founding a state which would advance Italy's freedom from foreign domination, and the *Discourses* shows the relationship between republican political institutions and military organization, *The Art of War* systematically articulates a positive program of reform formulated on the applied adaptation of primarily Roman military principles and institutions required to preserve and defend both princely power and republican liberty. Its inspiring reevocation of classical examples and themes, conscious manipulation of historical fact for persuasive intensification, and sometimes pathetic, urgently prophetic tone relate it to the method and style of Machiavelli's other writings. Yet *The Art of War* transcends military particulars to clarify many of his earlier political ideas. Its originality resides in the full expression of the indissoluble connection between the political and military life of a state.

## Machiavelli's Military Experience

Although Florentines cherished their independence, notably under republicanism, their pursuit of cultural excellence and their purported miserly dispositions prevented total commitment to the military defense of their political institutions and autonomy. Florentine civic pride depended to a great extent on preserving its worldwide reputation for cultural superiority. It mainly ignored the importance of military strength in sustaining the institutions and independence which would protect that cultural excellence. For Machiavelli, the unforgettable lessons of contemporary history attested to the influence of military factors on civic and political life. Florence's repeatedly unsuccessful efforts to conquer Pisa using the *condottieri*-mercenary system had resulted in domestic instability and loss of international prestige, especially during the Soderini government.

Machiavelli's political career from its beginnings to his final days was concerned with military matters. On July 14, 1498, he was appointed second Chancellor and Secretary of the Ten on Liberty and Peace (Ten of *Balía*), an executive group commissioned to oversee military and foreign affairs. It scrutinized the activities of the hired *condottieri* who were more interested in saving casualties, prolonging the war, and getting more money. These soldiers of fortune often used strikes, threats, blackmail, and treachery to protect and enhance their own positions. Machiavelli's early commissions involved negotiations with Jacopo d' Appiano and Paolo Vitelli, two of Florence's *condottieri*. The Vitelli experience demonstrated the extravagance and ineffectiveness of the *condottieri*. In 1499 he summarized his impressions in his first official paper, *Discourse Made to the Magistry of Ten on Pisan Affairs*. In the summer of 1500 Machiavelli gained direct knowledge of the military operations against Pisa. Following the failure of this attempt, Florence resorted to the conscription of soldiers from the *contado* rural areas under its jurisdiction. Machiavelli was commissioned with enlisting 2,000 *contado* troops to support the 3,500 mercenaries forming the bulk of the 1503 summer campaign against the rival city. Lacking adequate training, the troops in this campaign likewise failed. In 1504 the Florentines devised an ingenious but impractical and ultimately unsuccessful plan, with the collaboration of Leonardo da Vinci and Machiavelli, to divert the Arno and isolate Pisa from sea traffic. It was only after another disastrous campaign in 1505 that the Ten passed the ordinance (December 6, 1506) authorizing Machiavelli to raise a full fledged militia.[2]

Machiavelli's ideas on the militia attempted to correct the stereotype about Italians, as expressed, for example, by Cardinal Rouen in *The Prince*, 3, that Italians did not understand how to wage war, that they made poor soldiers unable to adapt to war conditions. Machiavelli's military experience demonstrated the need for strong political leaders to inspire and educate the citizens in civic *virtù* through the discipline and loyalty of a militia. As an instrument of political and civil reform and reeducation, the militia would protect the stability of republican institutions by checking individual aspirations for power.

Although the 1506 ordinance advanced Machiavelli's attempt to gain acceptance of the militia, it did not fulfill his ideal plans. It excluded Florentine citizens, drafting instead only farmers and peasants under its rule residing outside the city walls. The city rulers and dwellers remained suspicious of the potential for rebellion by these Tuscan farmers, so their movements were carefully controlled. Between 1507 and 1508, however, Machiavelli succeeded in swiftly mobilizing the militia. He not only administered the bureaucratic details of the enlistment, but also traveled the countryside soliciting men and observing their training. The militia's support of the mercenaries cut the Pisan supply lines and they were forced to surrender on June 8, 1509. Unfortunately, when the militia was called on to face the seasoned, well-trained Spanish soldiers of the Imperial forces at Prato in 1511, it suffered a catastrophic defeat and thousands of casualties, resulting in the fall of the Soderini government, the return of the Medici as rulers, and Machiavelli's removal from office and subsequent exile. Ironically, his brainchild, the militia, was responsible for the fall of the republican government and his own personal and professional tragedy. Ironically again, his hope to reenter political life during his last years was based not only on his writing of *The History of Florence*, commissioned by the Medici Pope Clement VII (1525), but also on his 1526 proposals to the Pope recommending strengthening of Florence's military fortifications. The report gained him appointment as secretary of the newly created Five of the Walls, to oversee the city's plan to renovate its defenses. Irony again persisted to color Machiavelli's final days. In May 1527, the republican party overthrew the Medici, Machiavelli again lost his position, and on June 21, 1527, he died just when it seemed likely that a new militia would be formed.

The controversy over the militia continued after Machiavelli's death, fueled by French threats to attack Florence and reinstate the Medici. The ordinance of November 6, 1527, authorized the conscription of soldiers from both the city and the *contado* under the direction of Donato Giannotti, a friend of Machiavelli who now occupied his mentor's old position with the Ten. Although the militia failed, and Florence fell in 1530, it did so only after a courageous defense, and among those who died was Machiavelli's son, Lodovico.

Machiavelli's military experiences form the basis of his ideas on the purpose of war and the most effective methods for its successful conclusion. Far from being a militarist, Machiavelli's advocacy of war is qualified by the political dimensions of his theories and vision of society. War is advocated to oppose external exploitation or to reform a deteriorating society following a period of successful conquest. Despite the bitterness of these military experiences, Machiavelli's writings on war reveal an ability to isolate political and historical problems and to propose principles and actions for their resolution. More than any writer of his time, Machiavelli perceived the influence of the military in the politics of sixteenth-century Italy and Florence, and for this justly deserves recognition as the first military theorist of modern Europe.

Influence and Sources

In *The Art of War,* as in Machiavelli's other writings, his military experience coalesced with his knowledge of classical and contemporary thought. The major classical sources of the work are Vegetius, Frontinus, Polybius, and Livy, in addition to the minor influence of Caesar, Josephys, Plutarch, and possibly Aelian Tacitus (Aelianus). The Latin title which Machiavelli used to refer to his work while writing it is derived from Vegetius' treatise *De re militari* (fourth century A.D.), a sourcebook on Roman military practices. *The Art of War* reflects Vegetius' five-part structure: I. selection and training; II. military organization; III. strategy and tactics; IV. sieges and fortifications; V. naval warfare (a topic Machiavelli does not treat). *The Art of War,* I depends on Vegetius and to some extent on Polybius for its principles on selection and recruitment; the training practices described in Book II rely on part two, Book I of Vegetius, while the description of Roman weapons and armor is drawn from Polybius. The unprecedented ideal battle Machiavelli describes in Book III may have been inspired by Xenophon's description in the *Cyropaedia* of the battle between Cyrus the Great and King Croesus of Lydia. The description of this remarkable battle redeems Machiavelli from any accusations of indiscriminate militarism, for as in Virgil's description of the bloody Sack of Troy, Machiavelli exposes war's senseless carnage and destruction. Vegetius' Book III is the fount of Machiavelli's discussion of tactics and leadership in Book IV, while his analysis of ancient military strategies refers to Frontinus' *Strategems.* Book V, dealing with the order of the march, corresponds to Book III in Vegetius, and although much of Machiavelli's encamping plans in Book VI are original, Polybius' *Histories* VI, 27–42, Vegetius, and Xenophon all treat this subject. Finally, *The Art of War,* VII assimilates Vegetius' ideas on sieges in Book IV. Machiavelli differs from Vegetius on the desirability of a professional standing army and on minor points regarding recruitment, promotion, weapons, combat methods, ordering of troops, and encampment. Yet Machiavelli's seeming dependence on Vegetius may account for modern neglect of *The Art of War.*[3]

Aware of the influential military treatises of Egidio Colonna (1247?–1316) *(De regimine principum)* and Christine de Pisan (1365–1430) *(Livre des faits d'armes et de chevalrie*, III, 7), Machiavelli was also imbued with the humanistic exaltation of Roman military excellence and with the appeals of famous humanists such as Petrarch (1304–1374) and Coluccio Salutati (1331–1406) for expulsion of foreign barbarians. The relative merits of mercenary forces versus those of the native militia had been argued throughout the 1400s. Writers before Machiavelli, such as Matteo Palmieri (1406–1475; *Libro della Vita Civile*), and Franciscus Patricius (1412–1494; *De institutione rei publicae)*, had discussed various military questions including the militia.[4] Although the lessons of history based on a study of classical sources inspired Machiavelli's war theories, as a pragmatic humanist he constantly attempted to discover and reevaluate past laws and adapt them to reform the contemporary Italian political situation. This did not protect him from errors in their application or in his reading of contemporary military developments. Far from impractical or quixotic, his synthesis of new military tactics with the Roman ideal reflects an assessment of the antiquated nature of the *condottieri*-mercenary system and of the value of the infantry, composed of responsible native citizens, in inspiring civic *virtù*, in preserving republican institutions, and in resisting foreign aggression.[5] Machiavelli's belief that the basic element of war—man—prevailed despite technological innovations is revealed in his praise of the ancients not only for their bravery and valor, but also for their systematic dedication to organization, discipline, and drill, aspects modern war theorists have adopted from Roman models. His war philosophy reaffirms the necessity to annihilate as well as exhaust, for war is a struggle both for political autonomy and physical survival. Such a struggle warrants all methods, strategic as well as deceptive, and the medieval chivalric courtesies and religious justifications of war which had persisted into the 1400s were outdated. Machiavelli's pragmatic deviation from his sources, therefore, is seen (1) in his unique advocacy of the popular infantry over the aristocratic cavalry, (2) in his deemphasis of artillery in favor of individual *virtù*, (3) in the combination of pikemen and short-swordsmen which had no classical parallel, (4) in his emphasis on the decisive battle in determining the outcome of a war. More importantly, Machiavelli's longstanding contribution is seen in the comprehensive and revolutionary way he relates military institutions, tactics, and advanced technology to an essentially secular but humanistic philosophy of war and to its political implications.[6] Machiavelli's use of Roman example, like his cyclical-spiral theory of history, often functions as a rhetorical, didactic, or satiric device by which he advances the need for present reform. His recognition of the decaying effects of material progress and new technology motivates his advocacy of the modern application of classical models, and in this light Machiavelli may be seen as a moralist.

## Structural, Thematic, and Rhetorical Analysis

In the preface Machiavelli dedicates *The Art of War* to Lorenzo di Filippo Strozzi, brother of Filippo Strozzi, husband of Clarice di Piero de' Medici and counselor of Duke Lorenzo de' Medici until the latter's death. Lorenzo had introduced Machiavelli to Cardinal Giulio de' Medici at the Orti Gardens on March 10, 1520. The dedication suggests not only Machiavelli's gratitude to Lorenzo for this introduction, but also his desire to reenter political life and to encourage acceptance of his proposals for reform. The dedication also reveals that Machiavelli's intention here, as in the *Discourses,* was to avoid dedicating his work to a prince.

Bernardo Rucellai, grandfather of Cosimo, had initially organized the Orti group during the early part of the first decade of the 1500s. The group's direction during this phase of its existence was to provide an outlet for the opponents of the Soderini government's policy of excluding aristocratic Florentines from political life. After Bernardo's death, Cosimo reorganized the group for primarily literary rather than political reasons. Machiavelli may have been introduced into the Orti in 1516 and was probably present when the *condottiero* Fabrizio Colonna visited the Gardens in the early fall of 1516, on his way to Rome from his triumphant war experiences in Lombardy.[7] Machiavelli's inclusion contributed to the group's new direction during this later phase, as indicated by the pedagogical intention motivating the entire *Art of War*. In dedicating the work to Lorenzo and in presenting it to the young Orti frequenters,

Machiavelli may have hoped to instruct them on the relationship between republican institutions and Rome's military effectiveness. This hope pervades the work, finding its summation in Fabrizio's last speech in Book VII. In lamenting his inability to realize his military reform proposals, he urges these men to seize the times and advise their princes on appropriate action.

Machiavelli's intention, expressed here and elsewhere in the work, suggests that the Orti discussions, and the artistic setting they provided for *The Art of War,* dramatized the link between practical politics and the humanist rhetorical tradition. The Orti setting synthesized a number of important aspects: the detached Platonic atmosphere where Socratic dialogue was employed for pedagogical intent; the humanist enthusiasm for all ancient Roman models; the practical demands of contemporary Italy; the impelling changes in warfare brought on by the new science and technology. The complex interrelationship of these factors must be evaluated in determining Machiavelli's accomplishment in *The Art of War.* Florentine civic humanism, epitomized by the Orti group and representing an important influence on Machiavelli's literary forms and political ideas, rejected nonapplied, theoretical, or technical speculation. *The Art of War* was not intended as a technical treatise on how to wage war, but was designed to reform the corrupted civic and military life by stimulating men's wills to initiate change.[8] Machiavelli invokes Roman antiquity in order to teach men and to spur them to achievement. The use of this paradigm, like the elegant expression, latinized phrases and other elements of humanist rhetoric, functions as a meaningful literary device in reforming the real world.[9] The idealized conventional portrayal of ancient, as well as contemporary, princes, republics, and generals is intended to influence the remolding of Italian political and military life. The significance of rhetoric's role in politics and warfare resides in the ethical foundations and educative goals which motivate its use in the renewal of civic aspirations. Both rhetoric and military training were viewed as political instruments, and as such any analysis of Machiavelli's *Art of War* must consider how his military ideas drew from politics and rhetoric, and how rhetorical methods are used in military analysis. Therefore, while in *The Art of War* Machiavelli eloquently aspires toward a renewal of political autonomy and liberty by a return to Roman military practices, an aspiration consonant with the Florentine humanist tradition, he also presents a pragmatic and technical assessment of the interrelationships of military and political efficacy based upon the direct experience of facts and theoretical reflection on events. In attempting to characterize *The Art of War,* it would be as simplistically misleading to conclude that military considerations are analyzed detached from all other social factors, as it would be to say that in *The Prince* politics is treated as an autonomous activity. The imaginative dimension of Machiavelli's vision of war, as in his vision of politics, helps to explain the fictionalized, caricatured battles, historical anachronism and distortion, and prophetic didacticism.

The preface to *The Art of War* brilliantly portrays this complex synthesis both in its style and thematic content. [10] Machiavelli addresses Lorenzo with the problem of how many have viewed civilian life as being different from military life. In elegantly balanced sentences using compound verbs and typical "either-or" constructions, Machiavelli first outlines the opposing view, why civilian and military life are different, and then defends their complementary nature and at times identity based on a careful examination of ancient ways. To demonstrate that good customs in a well-ordered state must be protected by the military, Machiavelli resorts to the analogy of how the rooms of a splendid, kingly palace ornamented with gems and gold would deteriorate if a roof did not protect them from the rain. In preparing for his point that the low opinion of soldiering results from the corrupt divergence from ancient military custom, Machiavelli employs a series of rhetorical questions emphasizing how lawgivers and military men have recognized the civic responsibility and loyalty which a disciplined military life inculcates. His belief in the possibility of reform founded on a return to ancient forms and methods of excellence derives from his experience and reading, knowledge he does not wish to waste in idleness. Although his decision to transmit with words what he had learned about war possesses the potential for error, he holds that the error possible from rhetorical education is less in its detrimental effect than that of those who err in presumptuous actions which often ruin their states.

Book I begins by praising the now dead Cosimo Rucellai as a good friend, dedicated citizen, and skillful poet. Although the work focuses on Fabrizio as the main expositor of military principles, Machiavelli's praise of Cosimo establishes a positive attitude toward the character who will function as Fabrizio's principal questioner in Book I. Dramatically, the scene is set for the entire work, the Orti Gardens just after a banquet. The participants, including Zanobi Buondelmonti, Battista della Palla, Luigi Alamanni, Cosimo, and Fabrizio, retire from the summer heat to the shade of some tall trees. Fabrizio questions his host on the names of these trees, Cosimo answering that the modern unfamiliarity with their names is not strange or uncommon, although the ancients would have known their names. This remark provides Fabrizio's lead into the subject of the excellence of the ancients. In metaphorical language Fabrizio asserts how Italy could have avoided ruin if it would have been

like the ancients in things strong and rough, not in those delicate and soft, and in those that are done in the sun, not in the shade, and to take their methods from an antiquity that is true and perfect, not from that which is false and corrupt. . . .[11]

Realizing how effective a written work can be if it possesses an oral character, Machiavelli announces that he will shift from the narrative style, in which speakers are identified each time with awkward tags, to the straightforward dramatic form, as in a play. By removing himself as an authoritative spokesman, Machiavelli achieves the dramatist's aesthetic distance and allows Fabrizio, a celebrated, heroic *condottiero,* to express views which undercut the system he represented and from which he had benefited. The main rhetorical device is the Socratic dialogue, well suited for the humanist propensity to discover the truth about matters open to debate, offering different alternatives or points of view, and not subject to concrete, irrefutable proof.[12] Fabrizio affirms the importance of Cosimo as the wise questioner in the quest for truth about a controversial or problematic subject.[13]

Once the work's form and rhetorical devices are defined, the
speakers return to the question of the ancients and moderns. The
contrast between the civilian and military life expressed in the preface
is implicitly reiterated by the isolated, tranquil atmosphere of the
Orti setting. Fabrizio remarks that the Gardens personify the modern
retreat from involvement in civic military life. Cosimo justifies his
grandfather's building of the Gardens, explaining that his grandfather seemingly abandoned the ancients because he lived in a corrupt
age which required conformity. To imitate the ancients would have
attracted attention and hostility. Cosimo's speech is laced with an
analogy about a naked man lying under the midday sun or in the
snow, and with three examples (similes), Diogenes, the Spartans,
and Fabricius, of people who in practicing discipline and severe
living methods attracted societal objections. Fabrizio explains that
the ancients should be imitated in humane methods, habits of mind
and living in harmony with contemporary life. Fabrizio advocates
two humanistic principles in imitation: emphasis on man, and
adaptability. He cites aspects of Roman civilization appropriate to
modern times: the organization of Roman republican institutions,
the rewarding of excellence, the appreciation of poverty, military
discipline, obliging mutual respect and love among citizens, and
advancement of public over private good. To do so would be
". . . to plant trees beneath the shade of which mankind lives more
prosperously and more happily than beneath this shade."[14] This
exchange is important for how it defines the work's literary form,
rhetorical approach, and functional setting, for the way it demonstrates how far the modern age had deviated from past excellence,
and for how the ancients should be adopted. Fabrizio established
the limits of his advocacy of Roman military models, while at the
same time reaffirming the interrelationship of the state's civic-
political health and military strength. Furthermore, in response to
Cosimo's inquiry about why he had not imitated the ancients, Fabrizio explains that the occasion had not presented itself, and we
learn later (Book VII) that by the occasion he means the possession
of a state.

The rest of Book I deals with the citizens' militia, as opposed to
professional or mercenary soldiers, as a solution to Italian military

decadence, with the function of the militia in a well-ordered state in peacetime and war, and with the physical and moral criteria for recruitment.

Book II focuses on equipment, training, and battle drills. It compares Greek, Roman, and modern weapons, noting the resemblance between the battle effectiveness of the Greek spear and Swiss pikes. By pointing out their relative defects, Fabrizio demonstrates the superiority of his ideal militia equipped primarily in the manner of the Roman legion. Fabrizio is often inexact about details and telescopes his citation of authorities without distinguishing various historical periods. He expounds on the superiority of the infantry over the cavalry and on training the soldier in speed, agility, and strength. These individual training tactics must be supplemented by collective battle formation training of the brigade composed of 5,000 to 6,000 men divided into ten battalions of 450 men each. Fabrizio specifies methods of brigade and battalion training, such as the solid double square, and other derivative variations, emphasizing flexibility, order, and adaptability.

The most interesting topic occurs in the final pages of Book II, when Fabrizio speculates on the reasons for a modern lack of brave, disciplined soldiers. These comments supplement what Machiavelli had already said on this subject in *Discourses* I, 1, 3, 6; II, Intro., 2; III, 1, 36. The ancients possessed more *virtù* because their republican institutions nurtured the development of many virtuous men, as seen in Europe which had more republics than monarchies, in contrast to Africa and Asia where no republics and only a few monarchies existed. Republics, like Rome, lived under threat of invasion and tyranny; therefore, they promoted military defense out of necessity which in turn generated *virtù*. War can be a positive force preventing foreign incursion and internal apathy. It is difficult to revive good order and discipline once abolished, and the Christian religion, unlike Roman paganism, contributed to this breakdown by promoting values inconsistent with military *virtù*. States often chose to live an indolent life, free from confrontation, struggle, or inconvenience, relying on *fortuna,* rather than contending with it for superiority.

Book III examines in detail the battle actions of an ideal army, demonstrating attack and artillery methods. Luigi Alamanni now becomes Fabrizio's interlocutor. Fabrizio's description of tactics, training, combat, weapons, and organization in this model battle synthesizes the best of ancient and contemporary methods and concretizes the theoretical discussion in the previous books. Machiavelli's contribution to the literature of warfare is partially evident in three specific ways in this remarkable Book: in the adaptation of the Roman legion, in the role of the decisive battle, and in the function of the artillery. He revives the idea of the Roman legion, adjusting it to contemporary contingencies, tactically organizing his 25,200-man army (24,000 foot soldiers and 1,200 horse soldiers, although Machiavelli actually deals with only one-half of this number) into four 6,000-man legions, with ten battalions of 450 men in each legion. Although these minor tactical units were an improvement over the disorganized medieval companies which presented a vulnerable single front to the enemy, it was still impractical and awkward and would undergo revision by later military theorists such as Maurice of Nassau and Gustavus Adolphus.[15] In Fabrizio's plan, ten companies occupied the front, six the middle, and four the rear so that the front force could fall back into the one behind as the battle progressed. The pikemen in each battalion held the exposed ranks and the shieldbearers the rear ranks; the artillery would be placed in the front and cavalry in the flanks.[16] The success of the three-wave attack relied on discipline and valor, resulting from good recruitment and training and obedience to chain command, among other qualities epitomized in the Roman legion. Machiavelli's idealized vision of the Roman legion is somewhat static, however, ignoring the modifications it underwent in various periods.

Machiavelli's second contribution is the vivid description of the imaginary battle, which deviates from Vegetius and other sources. As a high point in Machiavelli's reiteration of his persuasive aims and in his emphasis on the role of the decisive confrontation in winning a war, the battle occupies the rhetorical and ideological core of Book III and of the entire work. The two previous books treated the recruitment and training of men to prepare them for military action, and the topics of the subsequent four books deal with marching formations, encampment, and fortifications.[17] The battle description skillfully intertwines dramatic, emotional statements functioning as stirring battle calls, with exceptionally visual and auditory effects heightened by directive tags such as "You see," and "Observe." It is described from the point of view of a strategically positioned observer witnessing the scene from a distance, an experience both Fabrizio and Machiavelli undoubtedly had. Yet while mainly narrative in form, it previews the dramatic skill of the plays in the way Machiavelli sustains the effect of actual involvement in the events. The battle is an idealized painting of a military landscape portraying the best tactics known from ancient and contemporary example in their almost mechanistic perfection without any limiting practical considerations. The success on the audience of these rhetorical and persuasive methods is evident in Luigi's responses before and after the description. "Truly, Sir, I imagine this army in such a way that I actually see it and I burn with desire to behold it in action," Luigi excitedly comments. After the description, he responds dumbfounded, "You have won this battle with so much speed that I am completely astonished and so bewildered that I do not believe I could explain it well if any doubt did remain in my mind."[18] Fabrizio's intention was to expound on those battle methods which had proved militarily effective, but more importantly to inspire his audience, for the most part nonprofessionals, inexpert in military matters, with the desire to take up arms.

Despite the criticism Machiavelli has received for his apparent deemphasis of the artillery, it is here that he makes his third major contribution in the literature of warfare.[19] The discussion of firearms is initiated by Luigi's inquiry as to why Fabrizio permitted the artillery to shoot only once and retreat quickly. The basis of his argument is the same as that regarding the debilitating effect of Christianity on military *virtù*. Machiavelli focuses on the human factor in war, on the soldiers' intelligence, initiative, and courage, their mental and moral excellence, resolve, and heroism. The attitude toward the artillery, like that toward Christianity, is not one of inherent rejection, but rather of qualified reassessment. Both had reduced the ability to practice *virtù* and undermined the resolute mental state required of the good citizen and dedicated soldier. Machiavelli's attitude toward the artillery and toward Christianity stresses how religious fervor and intelligent use of firearms could enhance and intensify civic and military *virtù*, not replace it. Moreover, his opinion of the artillery is determined by the primitive stage of its development at that time and by its usual ineffectiveness in the open field where hand-to-hand combat prevailed. Despite its drawbacks, Machiavelli acknowledged its demoralizing effects and destructive offensive power which he thought could be countered by the rapidity of a determined infantry and vigorous cavalry. The mechanisms of technological warfare are always viewed, then, within a humanistic context which accounts for the parameters of practical warfare in those times, and Machiavelli does not theoretically speculate on the future of firearms. Machiavelli's military, as well as his political, theories are based on the universality of historical experience and on the psychological consistency of human nature in any age, rather than on isolated, specialized, scientific or technological factors relegated to uninvolved technicians. He succeeded in presenting a nonliterary topic with the rationality and theoretical consistency of the scientist, while allowing war to remain an art which challenged the total creative and cultural capacities of a man and a state.[20]

While Book III describes the military application of the aggressive methods of the lion, Book IV defines the deceptive methods of the fox. With Zanobi as the questioner, it discusses the disposition of the army, the selection of opportune battle sites, the exemplary tactics of Hannibal and Scipio, the strategies of encirclement, surprise, confusion, and how to make use of victory and defeat. The analysis of tactical planning before and after the battle and of the principles of effective military leadership concludes by showing the leader's role in preserving morale through oratory and religion. As examples from past and present history show, an eloquent general can inspire his men in the face of death with the enthusiasm and will to overcome superior military strategy and weaponry.

In Book V Fabrizio, with Zanobi still the questioner, discusses methods of crossing enemy territory, proposing that the army be disposed in the form of a square. He describes methods to counter attacks made from the rear, flanks, or from two or more sides. He demonstrates the necessity of exact maps of enemy territory and the importance of guides and reconnaissance techniques in avoiding ambushes, in fording rivers, in safe marching, in pursuit and escape. He advises on the disbursement of supplies and provisions and on the disposition of booty and pay.

Book VI proposes a new design for the encampment of the model army in the form of a square having wide streets and open spaces. The camp plan, utilizing ancient practices, is invariable wherever it is set up and is like a movable city. In describing the methods of quartering troops, Fabrizio speaks to Battista on the selection of the site dictated by considerations for health and provisions, on the importance of guards, on the need for vigilance and rigid observance of discipline. He also explores the importance of secrecy, dividing and conquering the enemy, tactics against the desperate enemy or for outwitting the enemy, and protection against mutiny and discord.

Book VII culminates both Machiavelli's original contributions to the technical side of the art of war and the work's rhetorical intention. A little more than one-half of the book deals with the techniques of besieging and defending cities, explaining how walls, moats, ditches, forts, castles, mining, bastions, and other devices assist or obstruct in a battle for a city. Machiavelli's ideas on fortifications against the artillery, anticipating the proposals he would write a few years later in colloboration with Pietro Navarro on this subject, derive from his direct experience in the Pisa campaigns and at Prato. They reflect how the practical dimension of war coalesces with man's creative capacities in overcoming brute power. He combines elements of the French rampart, an elevated embankment, with the bastioned wall *(baluardo* or *ritorte)*. Two walls would surround the city with a wide trench ($60' \times 12'$) between.[21] Despite what critics have said, Machiavelli here emphasizes the power of artillery, suggesting that walls no matter how great cannot withstand repeated artillery fire.

This didactic section is followed by a list of twenty-seven aphorisms, based on Vegetius and ancient military wisdom, which sum-

marize the rules of warfare. They not only reiterate many of the
work's practical suggestions, but they reemphasize the need for hard
work and training and the ability to recognize and seize the opportunity. Fabrizio reminds his audience that his selective classical
allusions were not intended to present a realistic, or precisely historical description of military practices, but rather were designed
to demonstrate methods that could be adopted to reform the present
situation. The reforming intention motivates his renewed condemnation of mercenaries and his praise for the success of the Swiss and
Spanish. It also inspires his analysis of the qualities of the good
commander. The concept of leadership Fabrizio outlines is dynamic
and creative, summarized at the end of this section by the analogy
of the sculptor who ". . . will never think he can make an excellent
statue from a piece of marble badly blocked out, but he can from
one still in the rough."[22] Fabrizio categorizes two kinds of generals,
one who leads an already formed good army, and one who must
demonstrate his energetic creative capacities by first forming and
then leading his good army, as Pelopidas, Philip of Macedon, Cyrus,
and others did. Italy in its present condition demands the second
kind. War, like politics, is conceived as a creative act, requiring
a new form, a rebirth not unlike the revival of art which flourished
at this time. The founder of a new civil and military order is,
therefore, like the sculptor. War remains an art because it depends
on the creative spirit for its success. The military art, like all arts,
requires reason, experience, knowledge, organization, flexibility,
discipline, and practice for its mastery. Such a concept envisions a
dynamic, optimistic faith in man's ability to accept reform and
change, a view of Machiavelli which balances the conventional idea
that he thought man was basically evil and recalcitrant to change.
Like his ideal army and his ideal battle, the ideal general is inventive,
prepared, and ready to seize the opportunity. Yet military success
relies on political support, and it is only a strong, effectual, active
prince with a great state and many men under his rule who can
bring the needed reform. The change cannot be a mere gesture; it
must be comprehensive and profound, involving a complete revo-
lution in the fabric of the society. Lives and mental attitudes, institutions and customs, must be altered and revitalized. The pleas

of these final pages echo more explicitly, ardently, and desperately the ideas of *The Prince* and the *Discourses*. Fabrizio ends this emotional survey of Italy's political and military condition by lamenting his ability to perceive what is needed, but his helplessness in implementing his knowledge. He can only hope that the young, gifted men he has addressed can transmit what they have just learned to their princes. Although *fortuna* has not granted Fabrizio the political entity whereby he could actuate change, his hope for the future resides in the nature of Italy herself, ". . . since this land seems born to raise up dead things, as she has in poetry, in painting, and in sculpture."[23]

## The Influence of *The Art of War*

Machiavelli's editing of the manuscript authenticates this work perhaps more than any of his writings. It was published twice in Florence during the 1520s (1521, 1529); five editions appeared in Venice (1540, 1541, 1546, 1550, 1554); and one in Palermo (1587).[24] As with *The Prince*, *The Art of War* attracted an early plagiarizer, Diego de Salazar's 1536 *Tratado de re militari*. Another Spanish version was published in Italy in 1541 by Francisco de Pedrosa, *Aqui comiença el libro primo delarte y suplimento remilitar*. . . . Two French translations appeared, Jehan Charriers' *L'Art de la guerre composé par Nicolas Machiavelli,* and Raymond de Beccarie de Pavie's *Instructions sur le fait de la guerre* (1548), a work initially attributed to Guillaume Du Bellay. The first English translation appeared in London in 1560 by Peter Whitehorne, to be reprinted in 1573, 1588, and 1905. Henry Neville included a translation of the work in *The Works of the Famous Nicolas Machiavel* (London, 1675), followed by editions in 1680, 1694, and 1720. The Ellis Farneworth translation was published in London in 1762 and again in 1775. Detmold includes a translation in his 1882 American edition of Machiavelli's writings. Allan Gilbert's 1965 edition of *The Chief Works* includes the most modern translation of this work. Translations appeared in Germany in 1623 and Russia in 1839.

The influence of Machiavelli's military ideas can be seen in Antonio Brucioli's *Dialoghi della morale filosofia* (1537), Aurelio Cicuta's *Della disciplina militare,* Montaigne's "Observations on Ju-

lius Caesar's Method of Making War" in his *Essays,* the Marshall
of Saxony's *Reveries Upon the Art of War* (1757), and F. Algarotti's
*Scienza militare del Segretario Fiorentino* (1791), among others.
Thomas Jefferson is known to have owned a copy. Despite its wide
dissemination and its influence in France, England, Germany, and
the United States especially during periods of national military crisis,
a comprehensive and systematic study of its place in the history of
military thought remains to be done.[25] Such a study should include
a comparative analysis of the relationship of Machiavelli's approach
to that of military writers before, during, and after his time, an
assessment of the traditional as well as the unique aspects of his
thought and method, and a recognition of the significant role played
by the political-military events and Renaissance rhetorical practices.

## Chapter Five

# Politics, Diplomacy, and Florentine Historiography

In May 1525, Machiavelli traveled again to Rome to present the completed portion of his *History of Florence* to the Medicean Pope Clement VII. Yet his concept of history had begun to germinate some forty years earlier, when, in June 1486, his father records in his *Diary* how he sent young Niccolò to retrieve from the binder's a freshly bound copy of Livy's *Decades*. This early contact with Livy was inspired by Machiavelli's lawyer-father, who undoubtedly was influenced by the fifteenth-century Florentine interest in the study of Roman history and literature. This humanistic proclivity for Rome's greatness and the present value of its lessons operates as the foundation of Machiavelli's idea of history.

Significant also to the development of Machiavelli's political and military theories as reflected in his historical writings is the fact that so early in his career he experienced firsthand diplomatic affairs in sophisticated court circles. In July 1500, Machiavelli was sent with Francesco della Casa to France for the first of what would become four separate missions to that country and whose total experiences would be summarized in a work written between 1512 and 1513 entitled *Ritratto delle cose di Francia* [Description of French Affairs]. This first French legation to the reknown court of Louis XII, ending in December 1500, was intended to resolve an imminent political problem—the complicated and chaotic situation resulting from the Pisan war and from the erratic behavior of the mercenaries—and to seek French aid in Florence's continuing and obstinate efforts to suppress Pisa.[1] More importantly for his potential role as political, military, and historical thinker, this experience brought Machiavelli face to face with one of Europe's largest and most powerful, unified states.

If the unstable behavior of the Florentine mercenaries during the Pisan war had solidified Machiavelli's military views, his first foreign diplomatic legation, as revealed in the twenty-eight official letters he wrote during his stay in France, opened his eyes to the operations of a centralized and efficient modern state that viewed political realities from quite a different perspective than that of Florence. The Tuscan city-state's political and military weakness painfully evident during the Pisa episode must have seemed magnified here in the presence of this powerful and diplomatically astute nation. It was probably during his observation of French skill in international politics that Machiavelli's ideas on force and power assumed more definite shape.[2]

During the fourteen years of his diplomatic service for Florence Machiavelli would go on over twenty missions abroad: four to France, two to the German court of Emperor Maximilian, two to the papal courts of Alessander VI and Julius II, in addition to many minor legations to Siena, Piombino, Forlì, Pisa, and others. The knowledge and experience he gained during these missions, especially to the three major European courts, would combine with his awareness of internal Florentine politics and his wide reading of classical literature to reinforce his insight into man's socio-political role, which Machiavelli concluded after much observation and thought, was quite apart from his private metaphysical or spiritual role. At first, his insights appeared untried, unsupported by authority and/or experience with court politics as, for example, in his early letter to Ricciardo Becchi on Savonarola's two final sermons. Later official experiences recorded in the *Legations* are transmuted into refined political and military precepts in *The Prince, Discourses, Art of War,* and the literary and historical works.

## History and Politics

A synthesis of dialectical dialogue between past history and present experience on the one hand, and of an adherence to a traditional literary form on the other characterizes Machiavelli's approach to the study of history as well as his ideas on political and military matters.

His two "historical" pieces, *The Life of Castruccio Castracani* and *The History of Florence,* reflect the assimilation of his early political and diplomatic experiences both foreign and domestic, his reading of classical models such as Xenophon's *Cyropaedia,* and his humanistic awareness of how his writings related to the well-established genre of rhetorical history. Modern scholars accustomed to the criteria of factual, unbiased, historical accuracy have often rejected Machiavelli's "untruthful" approach to history in *The Life* and *The History of Florence,* viewing these works either as compromises of his historical integrity in favor of artistic inspiration, or as written exclusively to patronize the "court" favor of the Medici, from whom Machiavelli was supposedly seeking employment after his 1513 dismissal from office. On the other hand, critics of Renaissance humanist historiography have not hesitated to reproach Machiavelli for generally falling short in the practice of that fashionable art, especially when compared to his paradigmatic predecessors.[3]

*The Life of Castruccio* has suffered from a similarly confusing plurality of critical opinions. Guarino calls it a "fictionalized biography," Prezzolini a "historical romance"; Ridolfi cannot decide if it is a political or a literary work, at one point saying that Machiavelli superimposed politics and poetry on history. Turri deems it a political romance, Hale "an historical fantasy," Russo a military story, and Voegelin "a mythical image."[4]

It is unfortunate that critics should be so preoccupied with classifying Machiavelli's works rather than discovering the various forces and influences which contributed to that distinctively attractive quality in his writing. Although categorization can and is a useful tool in attempting to understand the cultural achievements of any age, the Renaissance period, and Machiavelli's work, are better understood when approached from the point of view of synthesis. His theory and practice of history is an amalgamation of various elements rather than a reproduction or a repudiation of any single one. In assessing his contribution to the development of historical writing, it is more useful to trace the relationship between humanist rhetorical historiography as a theory, tradition, and actual practice and Machiavelli's foreign and domestic political experiences in shaping his method, ideas, and tone in *The Life* and *The History of Florence.*

Humanist historiography was based on the imitation of ancient models, on the notion of the identity of today with yesterday. Florentine views on historiography at the beginning of the sixteenth century were for the most part in accord with earlier humanist practices, but they took a more pragmatic turn. F. Gilbert, Gray, and others[5] have defined the concept of humanist rhetorical historiography advanced especially in fifteenth-century Florence, by those who held the positions of secretaries in the Chancellery, as for example, Leonardo Bruni (1427–44), Poggio Braccialini (1435–58), and Bartolomeo della Scala (1465–97). Machiavelli's position in the Florentine Chancellery linked him to the tradition of preserving and transmitting the fame, glory, and reputation of the city-state through the history form. In both *The Life* and *The History of Florence* he generally adhered to the conventions of this tradition. His work does not, nor was it expected to, present any original analysis based on new research; instead he focuses on imitating a classical form and a rhetoric which would enhance the civic, political, and military virtues and precepts he intended to project through their historical exemplification and to suggest how they applied to contemporary problems. Machiavelli's two histories reflect the characteristics and prescriptions which typify the didactic and moral intentions of the humanist historiographical scheme: (1) dependence on Roman models, such as Livy, for the form of organizing the history into books and of using speeches, and on more contemporary, indigenous sources for specific facts and content, with little alteration or innovation in the interpretation of events, (2) the memorable narration of events in an elegant and eloquent style stressing rhetorical and dramatic effect, (3) the use of speeches to exhort as well as to embody precepts and dramatize the importance of the individual (the military leader or the statesman usually) in shaping history, and (4) a concern for foreign affairs especially wars, in helping to project a high reputation for the state.[6] Roman historians such as Livy had pioneered the art of formulating "images" of Roman society which would serve both as immortalizations of its glory and as moral example for subsequent generations.[7] The fifteenth-century humanist historiographers of which Machiavelli was aware operated as "image-makers" for their city-states. The interdependence of humanistic historiography and diplomatic relations, or court politics, is seen in the fact that history was intended to impress foreign governments and increase national prestige, rather than to advance any Christian notion that Providence governed universal history. Historical writing thus underwent an irretrievable process of secularization. Yet *The History of Florence* differs from the previous aggrandizing humanist histories in that Machiavelli portrays the gradual decline of Florentine *virtù* as epitomized by unceasing factional struggles and obvious military incompetence.

Florentine historiography emerged with renewed vigor following the French invasion of Italy in 1494. The constitutional struggles Florence had experienced combined with the tragic results of Charles's invasion particularly influenced the Tuscan view of the function of historical writing at that time. Earlier humanist history was pedagogical in intention stressing moral significance, while the Florentine view after 1494 was more to derive political lessons of immediate practical use to the crisis of the moment. Although history, like all public writing of that age, preserved the literary and rhetorical qualities of the traditional form, it focused on the typical political principles demonstrated in the historical events which bore relevance to man's current political behavior, to the function of political and military institutions, and to the conduct of government.[8] The Florentine historiographical method, as seen in Machiavelli's work, reflected the relationship between politics and history. History vividly objectified political and military principles, exhorting the citizenry to initiate creative political reform in order to fulfill their humanistic identity.

Several qualities distinguish Machiavelli's view of history. He saw past history in terms of its relevance to the present, often seeming only to consider history as either Roman or modern. In interpreting and evaluating past events and figures, he deduces a perpetual repetitiveness in the historical process which the events of contemporary history verify. The repetitiveness is not identical in quality, since he also documents examples of unrelenting corruption which demonstrate a steady degeneration from the historical pinnacle achieved by Rome. The study of history is useful not only because of its cyclical nature, but also because its spiral decline demonstrates the immutability of man's evilness, the eternally self-interested motives behind human action, and the inevitable decline in man's ability to cope with the human situation.[9] These private ambitions, egoism, and quest for power result from a lack of *virtù* in the life cycle of a state as well as in individual men. In *The Prince* and the *Discourses* Machiavelli presents this same vision of history, but the focus is on how history demonstrates rules and methods of action as *exempla* assuring success to the leaders, while in *The History of Florence* he presents a broad vision of the evolutionary repetitiveness of history and how this repetitiveness reveals recurring patterns.[10] His cyclical-spiral theory of history saves itself from complete cynicism and pessimism by the notion of the possibility of ascent and renewal through the emergence of a political redeemer, another point of contact between *The History* and *The Prince,* where this notion receives its fullest development. The great historical figures which appear in these two works are portrayed as eternal symbols of political action, as paradigms of an immutable historical law, as universally recognizable actors in an apocalyptic drama.

## *The Life of Castruccio*

Machiavelli's biography of the Luccan warrior-tyrant, *The Life of Castruccio* (1281–1328), written while on an official mission to Lucca, was an exercize intended to prove his skill as historical image-maker to the Medici who could commission him as official court historian.[11] The apparent intention succeeded, for in Zanobi Buondelmonti's letter to Machiavelli of September 6, 1520, acknowledging receipt of *The Life,* Zanobi describes the positive reactions of Machiavelli's Orti Oricellari friends to what they referred to as "your model of history."[12] Buondelmonti, Alamanni, and his other Orti friends seemed unconcerned that Machiavelli had incorporated, invented, or altered facts; rather they praised his elevated style and rhetorical flourish. Although they questioned the necessity of all the sayings attributed to Castruccio, they accepted Machiavelli's statement of purpose at the beginning of the work:

I have chosen to bring him back to the recollection of men, since I have found in his life many things, both as to ability and as to Fortune, that are very striking.[13]

The work is written in the manner of Plutarch's peripatetic biographies with many reminiscences of Xenophon's *Cyropaedia* and Diogenes Laertius' *Life of Aristippus*. It projects Machiavelli's political and military ideas from *The Prince* and *The Art of War*. He stresses the importance of an Italian hero of obscure, humble origins who through his *virtù* could become the founder of a great state. He shows how *fortuna* prematurely thwarts his ascent toward glory and how the deeds of this man's great life could be most instructive in teaching resolute, responsible political *virtù*. He offers detailed descriptions of military expertise and stratagems and demonstrates why the infantry is superior to the cavalry.

The work opens with a statement on how great men often come from a low birth, being abandoned by their parents and exposed to wild beasts. The afflictions of *fortuna* show themselves early in the lives of excellent heroes. Imitating and combining elements from the stories of Moses, Romulus, and Cyrus, Machiavelli then recounts how Castruccio was found by a widow, Lady Dianora, the sister of Antonio Castracani, a priest. The couple decide to adopt the baby and name him Castruccio. The story tells how the couple hoped the child would follow the priestly vocation, but at age fourteen the boy, already showing a strong individualism, ". . . laid his church books aside and began to cultivate arms." He is then transferred to the house of General Francesco Guinigi, where he trains as a soldier. Guinigi later dies, leaving to Castruccio the custody of his son and the administration of his estate. Although Castruccio had gained eveyone's friendship, this increased status caused envy in the people. The narrative recounts Castruccio's encounter with Uguccione della Faggiuola d'Arezzo, tyrant of Pisa. The story emphasizes Castruccio's superior knowledge of military tactics as responsible for his defeat of the Guelfs. Uguccione, for whom Castruccio worked, becomes jealous because Castruccio had taken away his sovereignty, and has him arrested. The Pisans revolt and Uguccione is forced to release Castruccio, who then organizes his supporters and attacks Uguccione. The latter flees and finally dies in Lombardy. Through the use of exemplarism the remainder of the story similarly surveys Castruccio's life by demonstrating how his character, his military expertise, and political manuevering are revealed in various successful attempts to expand Luccan territory and power. His character portrays many of the qualities Machiavelli had cited in *The Prince* as essential to the successful leader. But as so often occurs with great men, *fortuna* frustrates his quest for ultimate success; at the age of forty-four he became severely ill with a fever resulting from exposure to a wind after a victorious battle and died. His deathbed oration and the long list of sayings Machiavelli attributes to him at the end of the work summarize many of Machiavelli's military and political ideas.

Machiavelli's account of Castruccio obviously cannot be called an accurate historical rendering, as, for example, might be argued for Niccolò Tegrimi's factual biography of Castruccio.[14] Tegrimi presents verifiable facts in his study of the evil effects of tyranny and reveals his sympathy for republicanism, while Machiavelli selects, omits, invents, and exaggerates in the mythographic creation of an artistic, idealized, and imaginary portrait of a legendary hero who might have been the restorer of Italy. Castruccio becomes a mythical prototype for the ideal Renaissance prince whose brilliant *virtù* operates as an ordering force in the chaotic political and military situation. His image and preserved memory is instructive to those in Machiavelli's contemporary Italian and Florentine scene. Although Machiavelli may have only intended to provide his Orti friends with an enticing sample of his abilities to write a history of Florence (Machiavelli does deal with Castruccio later in *The History of Florence*, II), the suggestive implications of his work extend beyond this immediate purpose to interesting points of relationship with his other writings, and even further to a more modern pertinence.

## *The History of Florence*

After about eight months since the idea may have first originated during Machiavelli's March 1520 visit to Cardinal Giulio Medici, who had taken over rule of Florence following Lorenzo's death, on November 8, 1520, Machiavelli received the contract issued by the Medici through the *Studio fiorentino* to write ". . . *annalia et cronacas florentinas, et alia faciendum*" at an established annual fee.[15] Machiavelli neither attempted an original interpretation of his sources nor researched the archives for new discoveries of information which might invalidate the old sources. He simply presents in a new form the well-known facts in his sources. Primarily, the sources he followed were: in Book I, Flavio Biondo's *Historiarum ab inclinatione Romanorum libri XXXI;* in Book II, Giovanni Villani's *Cronaca;* in Book III, he followed several sources, Marchionne di Cappo Stefani's *Istoria fiorentina,* Gino Capponi's *Ricordi* and the *Tumulto dei Ciompi* (also attributed to Capponi), Bruni's *Historiarum,* and Piero Minerbetti's *Cronaca;* in Book IV, Giovanni Cavalcanti's *Istorie fiorentine;* in Books V and VI, Cavalcanti, Biondo, and Capponi, in addition to Giovanni Simonetta's *Rerum gestarum Francisci Sfortiae XXXI;*[16] in Book VIII he uses a direct source in describing the Pazzi conspiracy, Montesecco, a purported conspirator. For the most part he follows one author at a time, does not use modern scholarly standards, and does not mention differing accounts or divergent reports of an event.

The structure of *The History* is as follows: Book I deals with the general events from the fall of the Roman Empire to 1434 focusing on the theme of decline and corruption;[17] Book II traces the specific internal history of Florence from its origins to the plague of 1348 and the expulsion of the Duke of Athens; Book III, ending in the year 1414 with the death of King Ladislas of Naples and, considered the most distinguished of the whole work, treats the destructive factions and internal struggles in Florence by contrasting them with the constructive, vitalizing role factions played in Roman civil life; Book IV continues the emphasis on Florentine internal affairs up to 1434 when Cosimo dei Medici returned from exile; Books V, VI, and VII interconnect foreign and domestic affairs in their treatment of the Medici rule in Florence to 1462 and general conditions in Italy and Europe, while Book VIII focuses on Florence under Lorenzo il Magnifico from the Pazzi conspiracy to Lorenzo's death in 1492. In imitation of classical models each of the books opens with an introductory chapter which announces the content of the book and presents general reflections.[18]

In the Preface to *The History* Machiavelli explains why he decided to begin his account with the decline of Rome rather than with the events from 1434. Initially, he had thought that Bruni and Poggio had dealt sufficiently with what had happened before 1434, but later realized that there were significant gaps. His interest in domestic history stemmed first, from his desire to illustrate the effects of factional struggles on the city's political life and to instruct future generations how past experience could help them avoid such mistakes, and second, to reduce the space available to deal with the Medici.

Machiavelli worked intermittently on the history for about four years until May 1525, when he presented the completed portion to Pope Clement VII. What Machiavelli presented was the work as we have it today covering events from Florence's origins to 1494 and he was interested in continuing Medici patronage so that he might finish the history. *Historical Fragments* exist which indicate that he had in fact begun work on the continuation of *The History*. He became preoccupied with other activities, however, and made no further additions to the work, and then he died in 1527, leaving it essentially incomplete.

Machiavelli was obviously aware of the workings of court politics even before the writing of *The Life* and *The History*. Despite any anti-Medicean feelings he may have harbored, it is likely that as early as 1516–17 Machiavelli may have turned to the writing of plays, the *Mandragola,* in the hope of gaining some of the privileges which playwrights seemed to be enjoying in the papal court of Leo X. It is difficult to ascertain to what extent and in what specific ways Medici patronage may have forced Machiavelli to modify his evaluations of Florentine historical events.[19] His concern expressed to Guicciardini in his letter of August 30, 1524 (". . . if I give too much offense either by raising or by lowering these things."[20]) and those purportedly made to Donato Giannotti (the subsequent owner of *The History* manuscript) attest to his sensitivity about the matter. However, despite the patronage, it is clear that Machiavelli's major intention is skillfully camouflaged by his literary and dramatic skills, such as the use of long speeches which embellish, affirm, and dramatize the significance of the historical event. Such speeches occur throughout, but are particularly evident in Book III; ch. 5 contains a long, anonymous oration on factions; ch. 11 presents Luigi Guicciardini's speech against disunion; ch. 13, a speech on the wrongs of the lower class; and ch. 23, Alberti's speech on his love for the city. He subtly presents an evolving image of how Florence moved from the heroic, military, republican virtues of her Roman origins and epitomized in the more contemporary, but unsuccessful figure of Rinaldo degli Albizzi (Book IV), to the values represented by the Medici who dangerously combined enormous personal wealth and mercantile know-how with a quasi-aristocratic or courtly facade, and extensive ties with foreign courts. Although the Medici may have thought that Machiavelli as "court" historian could do for them what Platina had accomplished for the Gonzaga or Merula for the Visconti, nevertheless, Machiavelli adroitly protected his originality of approach and integrity of interpretation by not beginning *The History* with the year 1434—year initiating the Medici reign—but rather with the city's Roman origins.[21] His analysis of the Medici usually appears in long eulogies, as for example those on Cosimo (VII, 5, 6) and Lorenzo, (VIII, 10, 36), which emphasize their importance to Florentine political and civic life and praise their personal qualities, rather than evaluate their method of rule. In Book VIII he focuses on the Pazzi conspiracy, and how it exemplifies the stupidity and ineffectiveness of conspiracies in general, rather than on whether their rule had been so tyrannical as rightfully to provoke such a revolt.

The extended analogy of the people on the plain and the prince on the mountain which appears in Machiavelli's dedicatory letter to *The Prince* affirms how aware he was of the difference in political vision between the prince or the aristocracy on the one hand, and the common people on the other. He speaks, not only in *The Prince* but in his historical works as well, from a uniquely authoritative position. In light of his personal republican heritage, he viewed history and the political lessons it reflected from a pole certainly different, if not opposite from that of the aristocratic, ruling class.[22] Books II and III trace the rise of tyrannies and the origin and outcome of revolutions by the cases of the Duke of Athens and the Ciompi, respectively. The gradual dissolution of the Medici court, with its emphasis on art and deliberate neglect of arms, as Machiavelli analyzes and portrays it in *The History,* combined with his personal experience with powerful foreign courts to strengthen his ideas on the ineffectiveness of the *condottieri*-mercenary system (VI, 1 as only one example) and the importance of forming a people's army. As he evaluated the relationships between causes and effects, immediate and longrange, the unparalleled reputation and respect artists and men of letters enjoyed in the Medici court had contributed to the decay of the Tuscan moral and civic fiber, to the neglect of military and political *virtù*, and to the general diminution of Florentine political power, an idea he specifically develops in V, 1. Moreover, these direct court experiences influenced the formulation of his more mature political theories, especially his awareness of the interdependence of political power and constitutional and military strength, and his special vision of the relationship between Florence's politico-military crisis and the overall Italian situation, particularly the lack of unity, direction, and leadership. The diplomatic missions had broadened his view of the various kinds of political entities and their potential for success. The unified territorial monarchies of France and Germany with their effective, well-organized military establishments certainly provided a threatening opponent for the fragmented, militarily weak Italian city-states and principalities. These foreign missions exercized his already skilled powers of observation and analysis, his knowledge of social and human psychology, his logical ability to reason on the causes and consequences of events. They heightened his perception and understanding of how the present came to be what it was during his time. In *The History* Machiavelli exceeds the boundaries of mere historian to become instead an artist-historian. His combination of cold logic and ardent passion juxtaposed with an intense awareness of inescapable ambiguities, ironies, and connections in the historical process accounts for one of the most personal, unique, and penetrating historical accounts ever written.

# Chapter Six

# Machiavelli's Dramatic and Literary Art

Dating, Manuscripts, Editions, and
Performance of the *Mandragola*

Although the action of the *Mandragola* occurs in 1504 (I, 1), its composition date remains controversial. Various dates have been cited by Tiraboschi (1498), Villari and Tommasini (1512–20), Renaudet (1523), Colimore (1504–12), and Ridolfi (January-February 1518). Ridolfi's speculations, having recently gained widest acceptance, are based on two points. First, in III, 3 the old woman who briefly converses with Fra Timoteo fearfully questions, "Do you believe the turk is coming over into Italy this year?"[1] Ridolfi argues that this popular fear, which probably began after Turkish capture of Otranto in 1480, was alleviated from 1504 to 1517 by the truce between the Venetians and Sultan Bajazeth II. It intensified in the early months of 1518 when the Turks resumed their attacks on Italy.[2] Second, in Ridolfi's study of the play's first printed edition, lacking a date and place of publication but probably done in Florence, he uncovered on the frontispiece the apparent remnants of the design of the Medicean arms, confirming his linking of the play with Medici patronage and the engagement of Lorenzo, Duke of Urbino, with Margherita de la Tour d' Auvergne in February 1518.[3] Bertelli's critique of this theory points out how this presumed composition date would have meant that the play was written in less than a month, giving even less time to the actors to learn their parts for its supposed performance on February 16, 1518. Bertelli also argues that the Turkish threat was constant during Leo X's reign and not limited to or intensified in the early months of 1518.[4] The 1518 date has been reinforced by Parronchi, who, in attempting to identify the three plays performed on successive evenings of Lorenzo's wedding festivities, assigns the *Mandragola* to the first day, September 7, 1518.[5] Ridolfi has also studied the only surviving manuscript of the play, Laurenziano-Rediano 129 (dated 1519), containing a rich collection of Lorenzo de' Medici's (Il Magnifico) poems. He has concluded that this manuscript depends greatly on a lost one, perhaps the autograph, that the 129 was copied one year after the play's composition, and done independently of the anonymous printed edition.[6]

The first recorded reference to the play appears in Battista della Palla's letter to Machiavelli from Rome on April 26, 1520; this reference together with a statement in Paolo Giovio's *Elogia illustrium virorum* (Venice, 1546) have been taken to mean that a performance was done in Rome for Leo X. Marin Sanudo's *Diarï* (1496–1533) records a second reference on February 13, 1522, recounting a performance for the Venetian carnival that year. A third reference in Vasari's (1511–1574) *Life of Bastiano Aristotele da San Gallo* suggests a performance in Florence sometime between 1524 and 1525 and that it was composed before *Clizia*. Other early performances are recorded by Giovanni Manetti in a letter to Machiavelli on February 28, 1525/26 (Florentine style), about a Venetian performance and by Guicciardini in correspondence with Machiavelli. It was for a planned performance Guicciardini organized in Faenza in 1526, but never executed, that Machiavelli wrote certain parts of the prologue and the songs which were inserted.[7]

## Setting, Plot, and Characters

The opening Canzone praises the advantages of the secluded pastoral life over urban involvement to be depicted in the play. Lamenting life's transitoriness in the face of which man can only seek pleasurable distractions, the nymphs and shepherds advise escape from this world's labors, anguishes, and deceits which ultimately crush all men. The Prologue is organized into two sections: the first describing the setting, characters, and plot and ending with reference to the play as a *badalucco* (joke, game, pleasurable sport); the second, focusing on the author and his relationship to his age—patrons, audience, and society. The speaker identifies the localized Florentine setting[8] and specifies the street as *Via dell' Amore* ("Street of Love"), from where, he warns, one can never rise once he has fallen. Admitting that the events to be dramatized are strange but true, the speaker identifies the protagonists, beginning with Messer Nicia whose study of *Buezio* (Boethius, with a pun on *bue,* meaning "ox," the symbol of stupidity), has gained him nothing but the horns of the cuckolded man. Callimaco Guadagni, whose last name means profit, will trick a beautiful, virtuous lady by means of his charm, fine dress, and courteous ways. It would, however, be a pleasurable experience for the audience to be tricked in such a harmless, painless manner. Alluding to the play both as a *favola* ("tale") and a *badalucco,* he identifies the four major characters: doleful lover, stupid judge, wicked friar, and evil parasite.

From this transition strophe the speaker commiserates with the uncelebrated author portrayed as neglected, unappreciated, and unrewarded, victimized by the present moral decline and degenerate separation from past cherished values. The speaker warns in the last three strophes that the author will not succumb to indiscriminate censure, since he, too, is skillful at the same art.[9]

The plot tells how Callimaco, exiled from Florence to Paris for twenty years, returns to his city upon hearing of the legendary beauty and exceptional virtue of Lucrezia Calfucci, the childless wife of a Florentine judge, Messer Nicia. Driven by passion, he enlists the assistance of Ligurio, a parasite, matchmaker, opportunist, and con-man, in devising the plan by which he hopes to possess Lucrezia. Aware of Nicia's vanity, foolishness, and provincialism, the conspirators devise a plan whereby they will propose to relieve Lucrezia's childlessness by administering a fertility potion derived from a mandrake. Callimaco, posing as a learned doctor, convinces Nicia of his drug's efficacy, but warns that its only side-effect is that the man sleeping with Lucrezia first after the potion has been given will die within a week. In several scenes which uncover Nicia's comic stupidity, Ligurio and Callimaco convince the easily duped Nicia to permit a substitute lover for that first encounter, who unknowing to Nicia will be Callimaco disguised as a street musician. Once reassured of his facile morals, the conspirators solicit the aid of Lucrezia's confessor, Fra Timoteo who, for the promise of an alms-offering, coaxes the unwilling Lucrezia to take the potion and sleep with a surrogate, if, as he is assured, the end result will be children. The Friar's casuistic arguments and the encouragement of her materialistic mother (Sostrata) finally induce Lucrezia. The potion is administered and Callimaco, disguised as the sacrificial surrogate, finally confesses the entire plot once alone with the lady. She accepts his love and pledges that he will become a permanent part of their new family. Everyone then goes off to church for the Friar's blessing.

## The Use of Sources and Traditions

Although the *Mandragola* is perhaps the most original play of the Italian Renaissance, it relates to classical and contemporary dramatic sources and traditions, a comparative study of which reveals Machiavelli's innovation and ways in which subsequent dramatists, Continental and English (Shakespeare not excluded), would build on the road he paved. During the fifteenth century a tradition of Latin comedy developed in Italy receiving impetus from the humanist revival of the ancient texts of Plautus and Terence. The discovery of classical texts and early critical commentaries, such as that by the fourth-century Donatus, along with the increased study, editing, translation, and circulation of printed editions resulted in the development of what came to be known as *commedia erudita* ("learned comedy") in the sixteenth century.[10] Its name derived from its erudite recollection of the Latin comic structures of Plautus and Terence, its composition by the humanist *letterati,* and its frequent performance before such literary court circles as Urbino, Ferrara, and Rome. These plays, of which Cardinal Bernardo Dovizi da Bibbiena's (1470–1520) *Calandria* (an adaptation of Plautus' *Menaechmi*) is the most influential, were lively, spontaneous, and satiric representations of the social life of the times. Often they ironically juxtaposed learned, aristocratic views with more simple, popular elements. Basically they imitated classical form, assimilating and adapting classical themes and character types to contemporary and local concerns.

*Mandragola* imitates classical structure in its simple, direct, uni-
linear plot organization (*protasis, epitasis,* and *catastrophe,* with *par-
askene,* or transition scenes) and its observance of the unities of place
and time even before they were formally authenticated in Renaissance
critical theory.[11] Yet the play is more remarkable in how it deviates
from classical models. Written in Florentine idiomatic prose, it
mirrors a localized setting and texture as well as the unique Florentine attitudes and temperament. The language and gestures that
might have accompanied it imprint a memorable picture of Renaissance Florentine customs. Machiavelli's insertion of *intermedi*—
songs between the acts—also deviates from classical structure, while
his thematic exploration of marriage as a sacrament and social in-
stitution reflects a new attitude on appropriate dramatic subjects.
Finally, in noting Machiavelli's debt to or divergence from traditions, we need to mention that in its cynical characterization, its
prose tale narrative form, and in its emphasis on trickery and sen-
suality, *La mandragola* reverts to Boccaccio's *Decameron.*[12]

## Dramatic Literary Analysis

A survey of the critical approaches to Machiavelli's plays verifies
how a thoroughgoing analysis of his dramatic techniques, symbols,
themes, language, and imagery has taken second place to the power
of his ideological vision. Yet fascination with that vision derives
largely from such devices. The plays, like the political works, break
through the cultural confines of Machiavelli's intellectual world.
Some have approached the *Mandragola* as a dramatic portrayal of his
political theories and maxims, a dramatic version of *The Prince* and
*Discourses,* written possibly as has been said of the former, to gain
the Medici's political favor. This view is reinforced by the play's
association with Lorenzo de' Medici's marriage in 1518. Similar is
the approach which sees the play as a political allegory of contemporary historical figures and events intended to suggest solutions
to current political problems.[13] Although Machiavelli's plays reflect
the political thought, historical vision, stylistic modes, and syntax
of his major works, they possess an artistic integrity of their own.
They reflect Machiavelli's psychological power and the caustic commentary on social, moral, and political chaos in his political writing.

The plays also show how *virtù* can overcome *fortuna*. Yet *Mandragola* remains of interest for its dramatic and literary dimensions, not for how it reflects the author's politics. Criticism from the 1500s to the 1700s indicates acceptance as typical of Renaissance adaptation of dramatic sources, traditions, and conventions. The audiences ignored Machiavelli's increasingly tinged reputation deriving from a distortion of his politics; in fact, the play's popularity increased while his political works suffered. In the 1800s there was more concern for the bitter tone, the portrayal of corruption, the satiric intention, until in the early twentieth century Benedetto Croce saw in it Machiavelli's secret desire for an ideal society.[14] An analysis of Machiavelli's plays must consider their place within his entire canon, recognizing them as another expression of a unified vision of man and the world, while also acknowledging them as discrete, artistic entities. Such a balanced approach will give proper weight to the role of ideology and art, it will recognize the dramatic and rhetorical element in all his writings, and will heal the so-called dichotomy between Machiavelli as thinker and as artist.

*Mandragola*'s excellence emerges from its comic spirit, psychological characterization, brisk unfolding of plot, and stylistic directness. It is perhaps one of the first plays to assimilate such political ideas as conspiracy, policy, *fortuna* versus *virtù*, ends justifies the means, and others in the comic portrayal of marriage and seduction. While Machiavelli's political writings have been recognized as a source of the English stage Machiavel, little if any study has been given to how his comic characters and themes may be the source for those in Shakespeare and other English and continental playwrights.[15]

The Prologue to *Clizia* and the *Discourse or Dialogue Concerning Language* (1514–16) provide important insight on the criteria governing *Mandragola*'s comic effect. *Clizia*'s Prologue affirms the recurrence of analogous comic events in all ages; thus, the justification for the updating of classical sources and their contemporary Florentine localization for the audience's greater pleasure. While admitting the need to camouflage the identity of the Florentine citizens to whom the dramatic characters may relate, the speaker categorizes seven comic types and one general theme as the stuff of comedy: an old man's avarice, a lover's madness, a servant's tricks, a parasite's gluttony, a poor man's distress, a rich man's ambition, a harlot's flatteries, all men's unreliability. The purpose of comedy is to benefit and please the audience, ends which can be fulfilled by the use of model instances, persons, and language which incite laughter. Language, which reflects character, is what provokes laughter and it must be stupid, sarcastic, or amorous, projecting characters who are foolish, malicious, or in love. In his *Dialogue Concerning Our Language* Machiavelli provides additional information on his theory of comedy and its basis on the use of native, dialectical language, preferably Florentine, which he considered the fountainhead of the Italian language. Comedy is defined as a mirror of private life treated in a ridiculous manner. Examples of human nature (the fraudulent servant, silly old man, young man crazy with love, flattering whore, gluttonous parasite) provide practical models. Machiavelli's critique in this *Dialogue* of Ludovico Ariosto's play, *I suppositi* (1509), while praising the plot as "a knot well tied, but better unravelled," reproaches Ariosto for failing to employ appropriate comic language. [16] The characters and plot acquire their comedic effect through the mask of a highly expressive Florentine dialect. They are rendered laughable by their language, not by their nature, which if projected through a different language might make them pathetic or tragic. [17]

The play reveals qualities traditional to comedy. Although there are constant references to death and the use of death imagery, particularly in association with Callimaco's self-consuming passion, unlike the tragic portrayal of love and death in *Romeo and Juliet,* the trickery here is painless as the Prologue to *Mandragola* carefully points out. It ends not in death, as the use of the potion promises to the first man who sleeps with Lucrezia, but rather in renewed life and reconciliation projected by the traditional symbol of comedy, marriage. It is a comic treatment of legal marriage (Nicia is a doctor-in-law), ending in the religious and social sanctioning of a false marriage. The implications of this satirically corrective contrast are seen in Callimaco's impersonation as a physician and in the inverted use of the mandrake as a curative and regenerative agent. The Canzone preceding the play implicitly contrasts romantic comedy, which avoids mirror reflection by leading the spectators into an imaginative, timeless, dream world often pastoral, and critical social comedy which mirrors the errors and ridiculousness of urban life. The contrast is seen in the language used to draw these different worlds: the first, elegant, idealized, formal; the second, dialectical, realistic, informal. While in tragedy the rhythm of life is stifled by change and chance, here there is a triumph over *fortuna* by adaptation to and exploitation of circumstance through plotting and deception.[18]

Callimaco's language reflects three thematic trends: (1) the political maxims associated with Machiavelli's other writings (I, 1); (2) the humanist concern for the elegance of Latin syntax (II, 2); and (3) the conventional Petrarchan/courtly expression of love (IV, 1, 2, 4). The soliloquies in IV reveal how the "war" on Lucrezia's modesty suggests a repressed association between love and death, and as the seduction nears love's potentially fatal symptoms are boldly drawn. Callimaco's language is especially interesting since in IV, 1 he ironically desires to possess the virtuous without regard that in so doing it will ultimately be debased. In IV, 2 there is an ironic contrast between death and the fertility/birth which the union promises. In courting Lucrezia, Callimaco likewise courts death and in IV, 4 as the union approaches he threatens suicide as a substitute for sexual fulfillment if the plan fails—death by drowning, hanging, jumping out a window, and stabbing. Callimaco's success in executing his plan derives from his *virtù*, his good fortune, his realistic hope based on an accurate assessment of the risks. The Canzone at the end of I accentuates the theme of hope and fear which Callimaco reflects. Lucrezia's defeat, effected not by forced rape, but by trickery, exposes the traditional courtly-chivalric adulation of woman as merely a strategic camouflage of raw sexuality. Callimaco's peaceful conquest creates a new order with a minimum of violence and pain.

Ligurio's language is direct and rational in its efficient evaluation of the circumstances, risks, and probabilities. He exposes the disproportion between talent and reward in his perceptive evaluation of Nicia's stupidity and his fortuitous rewards (I, 3), and clearly perceives what motivates a reputable friar to evil (III, 1). Ligurio's characterization possesses traits of the conventional court panderer and jester; however, his acrobatics are mental rather than physical. Nicia's stupidity is reflected in his idioms, proverbs, infantile expressions, and obscurities. He is a pedantic, myopic, and provincial simpleton who easily agrees to his wife's seduction after he learns that the French king used the same method to cure infertility. His singleminded concern for a child is celebrated in the Canzone that ends II. In II, 3 he presents a self-condemning national character sketch of Italians (*ritratto*) which laments their ingratitude, skepticism, and bureaucracy, and implicitly suggests the root of Italy's perennial cultural, political, and intellectual problems. Timoteo's language is venal, mechanical and formalized, objectifying his superficial concern with the exteriors of religion, with preserving appearances through the manipulation of rites and practices (V, 1). Timoteo recalls the anticlericism in Machiavelli's portraits of Savonarola (March 9, 1498, letter) and of the Franciscan preacher (December 19, 1513, letter) which epitomize the religious corruption, materialism, and immorality he so often condemned. Timoteo's narrowness, greed, and cynicism are reflected in his commercialized, utilitarian attitude toward religion based on the theory that good intentions justify everything. His shocking misogyny (III, 9, 11), combined with his sublimated eroticism and sexual fantasizing on the nocturnal activities of Lucrezia and Callimaco (IV, 10), mortally undercut Lucrezia's validity as an apotheosized model of virtue. His disguise as Callimaco for the purpose of fooling Nicia further reinforces him as a corrupted model, as a symbol of spiritual and sexual sterility. The Canzone on the sweetness of deceit ending III sums up Timoteo's character. Finally, it is Lucrezia who more than any other character demonstrates how disordering foolishness and trickery become the normal order of things. Throughout, the play juxtaposes the real world—how people actually live—with an implied ideal vision—how people ought to live in a world in which everything has its proper order and degree. In surrendering her body Lucrezia surrenders her integrity and commitment to an ideal order, illusionary symbols of the way things ought to be. A new hierarchical order with recategorized priorities is created out of the subversion and debasement of the old. Nicia is replaced by Callimaco whom she wants to be her whole world she says in V, 4—lord, master, guide, father, defender, and chief good. Cleverness, stupidity, folly, and greed—which characterize how people really live—become sanctioned as the new norm of how people ought to live. Through Callimaco, her new spokesman and mentor, Lucrezia affirms finally (V, 4) that the unequivocal and impelling success of his plan proves it must be God's will that she accept this new order.

## Dating, Manuscripts, and Performance of *Clizia*

*Clizia* was probably written during the last months of 1524 and January 1525. Although no autograph manuscript has been found, three copied manuscripts exist: the complete *Riccardiana* 2824, the incomplete *Archivio Boncompagni,* COD. F. 11, and the Colchester-Essex Museum manuscript discovered by Beatrice Corrigan in 1958 representing the earliest surviving version of the play, twelve years earlier than the first printed edition in 1537 by Maciochi. Corrigan's study of this beautifully illuminated manuscript identifies the scribe as Ludovico degli Arrighi, a well-known Roman calligrapher and printer, sets its date as 1525, and theorizes that it was commissioned as a gift for the marriage of Maria di Filippo Strozzi with Lorenzo Ridolfi. Machiavelli's close association with the two families, his 1525 presentation of *The History of Florence* to Clement VII in Rome, at which time it is thought Machiavelli spoke to Arrighi about doing the *Clizia,* and its linguistic features which suggest that Arrighi copied it from Machiavelli's hand, support Corrigan's association of this manuscript with the Strozzi-Ridolfi marriage. Although the marriage did not occur until 1529, Corrigan argues that Machiavelli's letter to Guicciardini, probably written in December 1525, shows that the union had already been contracted.[19]

Although the Colchester-Essex manuscript seems connected to the Strozzi-Ridolfi marriage, the play's composition may have been motivated by Machiavelli's desire to repay the generosity of Jacopo di Filippo Falconetti, called *Il Fornaciaio.* Falconetti owned a villa outside Florence where he entertained guests, Machiavelli among them. To celebrate the end of a five-year banishment from Florence, Falconetti held a series of festivities during which *Clizia* was performed on January 13, 1525. The stage scenery was done by Bastiano da San Gallo and the *intermedie canzoni* were sung by Barbara Raffacani Salutati, a young professional singer with whom Machiavelli, even at age fifty-six, was romantically involved. This love affair gives the play an autobiographical flavor since the plot of *Clizia* deals with an old man's love for a young girl.

## Setting, Plot, and Characters

Nicomaco, an elderly married Florentine merchant who had led an exemplary life, falls in love with Clizia, a poor, young Neopolitan girl. Clizia, orphaned during Charles's Italian campaign in 1494, was left at Nicomaco's home by a military officer who had found the five-year-old child in Naples. Clizia, now a young woman, was raised like a daughter in Nicomaco's house. Nicomaco schemes to marry Clizia to his farm servant Pirro so that he may himself enjoy her, since, as Cleandro, Nicomaco's son, explains, to possess her before her marriage seemed wicked and repulsive. Cleandro and his mother Sofronia, after discovering Nicomaco's plan, conspire to thwart his designs. Cleandro also loves Clizia, but her lowly birth and lack of dowry forbid their union. Cleandro decides the best he can do is to have Clizia married to his manservant, Eustace. Although he does not say so, the implication is that he hopes for the same privileges his father envisioned. Sofronia assists Cleandro, not to favor her son's unspoken designs, which she suspects, but rather to cure her husband of his amorous madness. Sofronia agrees to her husband's request to submit the question of whom Clizia should marry to resolution by lots. Nicomaco wins and prepares to execute his plan; however, Sofronia and Cleandro have not given up. During the wedding ceremony Siro, a house-servant, is disguised as Clizia. Once the couple has retired to the house Nicomaco had so generously prepared for them, Nicomaco enters the bedroom, is attacked by the "bride," and finally discovers Sofronia's debasing joke. Although mother and son have won, things seem hopeless for Cleandro, until suddenly a rich Neopolitan gentleman arrives announcing that he is there to claim his daughter Clizia. In his desire to repay Nicomaco's family for their generosity, he offers the now worthy Clizia in a marriage-alliance to Cleandro.

The Prologue describes the localized setting of the events which the speaker avows are true but admittedly stranger than fiction. It summarizes the plot as a rivalry between father and son over the possession of a girl. The characters are introduced by having the actors come on stage for presentation to the audience. The Prologue's two-part structure, similar to that of the *Mandragola*, extends its traditional function by then announcing Machiavelli's theory of comedy (already discussed).

## The Use of Sources and Traditions

*Clizia*'s source is Plautus' *Casina*, which in turn was based on the Greek play *Cleroumenoe* [The Lot Throwers] by Diphilus of Sinope, a dramatist representing the Greek New Comedy flourishing from 330 to 150 B.C.[20] Although Machiavelli's dependence on sources is minimal, the plot's derivative nature has hampered analysis and appreciation of the play. While Machiavelli imitated the Plautine use of entrance and exit announcements, asides, and eavesdropping incidents, for the plot he only used the actions from *Casina* II, 4 for the basis of *Clizia* III, 5, freely adapting rather than literally translating. There are a number of scenes and plot subtleties not in the source.[21] Machiavelli's characterization is also more realistic and full-bodied. He adds characters such as Cleandro who has an important thematic function of dramatizing the conflict between father and son and of portraying the effects of love (I, 2; III, 2; IV, 1; and V, 5). Cleandro also differs in that, unlike the Plautine source, he does not conspire with his servant to share Clizia for whom he seems to have a sincere passion. Nicomaco, unlike Plautus' Lysidamus, possesses many dimensions. Sofronia's soliloquy in II, 4 portrays a previously wise, dependable, and dignified father and husband, who was suddenly stricken by an amorous disease. His comic role, unlike Nicia's, is deepened by his pathetic, sincerely contrite return to his origins following his humiliating cure. Sofronia exceeds Plautus' caricature of the Roman matron in Cleustrata. Sofronia dominates the play as an exponent of, not only her sex and role, but also of the play's social and ethical themes. Her exposé of Nicomaco is motivated not by vindictive jealousy, but by concern for her husband, for Clizia's welfare, and for doing what is right to preserve the family. Her maternal tenderness toward Cleandro excludes indulging her son in order to punish her husband. Her forgiveness of Nicomaco is as sincere as his contrition. Critical neglect and appreciation of *Clizia* also derive from the stronger emphasis placed on *Mandragola*'s overall excellence. Enforced by Machiavelli's conscious paralleling of the plays in *Clizia* II, 3 when Nicomaco alludes to Fra Timoteo, Lucrezia, and Nicia, both plays are similar in their focus on the family and in their symbolic use of marriage as a reconciling force. In several ways *Clizia* is superior to the *Mandragola*. Its picture of daily urban Florentine life, its markets, pharmacies, househelp, bourgeois values, etc., is more genuine, vivid, and complete, its dialogue imbued with a more subtle sense of the ironic and unknowingly self-revealing. The roles are developed through longer speeches and more extensive exchanges between characters. It boasts several memorable scenes which embody major themes and contribute to its unique effect, as the throwing of lots and Nicomaco's simultaneously comic and pathetic account of how he was deceived.

Machiavelli's psychological penetration is revealed in the multileveled moral and ethical implications of *Clizia*'s themes. The play's rich texture of themes is expressed by means of an interwoven network of similes and metaphors. While the *Mandragola* uses native Florentine dialect for its unique comic effect, *Clizia* synthesizes that dialect with a variety of poetic imagery giving the play its quality of a true *commedia erudita*. Lovers are portrayed as lamenting bores (I, 1), the amorous situation is compared to a woman (IV, 1), and the unlucky man to a drowning sailor (V, 5). As in the *Mandragola*, history is used as a backdrop for the personal situation, but Cleandro's account of Charles's invasion of Italy with its attendant plundering and orphaning of children like Clizia is tragic in its overtones. The tragic dimension inheres as well in the themes of the potential ruination of a family (I, 1; II, 4), the inescapable physical effects of old age (II, 1; IV, 4), the waste of effort, talent, and virtue (II, 3), and most importantly the extravagant dissipation of a sensible, ordered life to pursue a self-indulging sexual madness (II, 3) masking as love. Each of the five *canzone* in the play portrays love in all of its romantic forms, effects, deceptions, and lessons. The effects of Nicomaco's disordering passion emphasize how the natural (the humors) and social realms are interdependent and why his punishment must be explicitly social as well as personal. Sofronia

is not only the spokesperson for the necessary harmony between the
personal and the social, but she is also the instrument for the administering of a required cure which will return her husband to his
original values after a fantastical period of deviation, and in so doing
reinstate the proper hierarchy of social values. The nature of the
medicine she administers represents the most important theme in
the play. Nicomaco's *ritornare al segno,* return to his origins, is
achieved through society's participation—family, servants, and
neighbors—in his derisive public shaming which simultaneously
purges Nicomaco of his personal disease and society of any propensity
for a similar disorder. Sofronia's explanation in V,3 emphasizes the
need for witnesses, for social participation in the condemnation of
Nicomaco's disease and in the approbation for his return to his old
self, for ". . . to err and to do better is common."[22] As Nicomaco
is exposed, the characters and audience laugh, and the laughter is
doubled and redoubled with each recounting. Various forms of the
word *ridere,* to laugh, pervade the final scenes. Nicomaco's seeming
*sciagura,* tragedy, is viewed in its true perspective as a comic epiph-
any of man's vain delusions. Rather than through demoralizing
invective, Machiavelli conveys his comic purpose and in turn his
moral through the theme of laughter. Unlike the ending of *Mandragola* which undermines traditional values to be replaced by a
revolutionary order, *Clizia'*s ending affirms a positive moral order.
Yet its dimensions have undergone a realignment, for it is now
Sofronia, not Nicomaco, who will establish the new limits governing
his future behavior.

## Machiavelli's Ascent of Mt. Helicon

While the plays have sometimes been studied as dramatic literature with a value and integrity of their own, the most common
approach by those who even bother to discuss Machiavelli's poetry
is as a tool in interpreting his political writing.[23] A study of the
Machiavelli canon affirms how he used his literary skill and imagination for political statement. The literary dimension permeates
and illuminates all his writings, and his inspiration came as much
from Ovid, Dante, and Petrarch as it did from Livy and Polybius,
as is evident from his December 13, 1513, letter to Vettori and

from the many allusions to these writers throughout his works.[24] Yet when one turns to his verse after an intense study of his political and historical writings, there is an undeniable disappointment. Machiavelli's poetry is the poetry of political idea and statement rather than the poetry of transcendental vision. Although it possesses the same imaginative scope, universal quality, and verbal power of his prose writings, it lacks the fiery passion, musical rhythm, and inspired visionary odysseys that are associated with Romantic conceptions of poetry. Tusiani has rightly noted that Machiavelli's poetry is different from much of that of his age;[25] however, it may be in this difference that distinguishes his poetic originality. Just as Machiavelli forged new ground in political writing, so his poetry seems to anticipate and to have more in common with the age of Dryden or Pope when emotion and suggestion were subordinated to reason and statement in poetry and when history and politics were often the primary subjects of memorable poetical treatments. The similarities of Machiavelli's poetic approach to that of the late seventeenth and eighteenth centuries require careful consideration, and in general it deserves more critical attention on its own terms.

*Decennali* [*The Decades*].    The two *Decennali* are historical poems, written in 550 lines of Dantean inspired *terza rima,* chronicling events in Europe of concern to Florence. The *First Decennale,* written supposedly in about two weeks in the autumn of 1504, covers the years 1494 from Charles VIII's invasion to 1504, and reveals the keen ability not only to characterize current history, but to see causal interrelationships. This *cantafavola,* as the genre was referred to, represents Machiavelli's first published work, printed by his chancery assistant and editor Agostino Vespucci in 1506.[26] It is dedicated to Alamanno Salviati, who had saved the Republic during the Arezzo rebellion and had stabilized the Florentine government by providing that the *gonfaloniere* hold office for life.[27] Yet, Machiavelli's use of the second person plural when speaking of Florence's disastrous Pisa campaigns suggests that he may have been addressing the Florentine people. Following its definition of the epic question and the invocation to the Muse, the poem rapidly and vividly narrates how Italian disunity promoted the barbarian invasions and how Florentine factionalism combined with its undermining dependence on France caused its political and territorial disintegration. Machiavelli's brief allusion to Savonarola (ll. 157–66), his skillfully drawn analyses of Louis XII of Orleans, Alexander VI, and Ludovico Il Moro, and his more extensive portrait of Cesare Borgia's rise, conquest of Romagna, and fall (ll. 289–475) exemplify his ability to transmute political events and historical figures into powerful, energetic poetry. While he carefully camouflages reference to specific Florentine personalities by the frequent use of symbolic animal imagery, he is unrestrained in his Dantean condemnation of the city, in the tirade against French ambition, arrogance, pride, and exploitation. The poem ends with vacillation between fear for future wars and hope that the adroit steersman, Piero Soderini, whom Machiavelli exhorts, can by Florence's development of its own citizen army, repel foreign invaders and prosper internally. By so doing it could avoid the past mistakes of dependence on such traitorous *condottieri* as the Vitelli, whose activities the poem outlines, and the self-destructive foreign and military policy which Florence's Pisa campaigns exemplified.

The *Second Decennale* planned to cover events from 1504 to 1513, but abruptly ends after 214 lines with the 1509 retreat of Emperor Maximilian from Vicenza, following his exclusion from the League of Cambrai. The League, composed of Pope Julius II, who had promoted it, Spain, the Empire under Maximilian, and France, was intended to destroy Venice. While the power of the *First Decennale* derives from Machiavelli's shrewd, passionate analysis of how external events and internal weaknesses affected Florence's political situation, the *Second Decennale* continues the perceptive analysis but lacks the fiery involvement and exhortative tone.

*Capitoli.*  The *Capitoli* on ingratitude, fortune, ambition, and opportunity, perhaps Machiavelli's most mature political poems, are inspired not so much by the contemplation of history but rather by the pertinence of his personal experiences to a larger historical context. The *Capitolo on Ingratitude* dates between 1507–15 and is dedicated to Giovanni Folchi, one of the Boscoli conspirators against the Medici. The opening lines establish the interrelationship of ingratitude and envy and self-define Machiavelli's poetic limitations. As in the dedicatory letter to *The Prince,* Machiavelli dramatizes himself as occupying the valley below the high mountain of poetic glory, Mt. Helicon, looking upward but never hoping to scale its heights. He merely hopes to gather tiny buds at the mountain's base, to employ his poetic art to vent his sorrow over his afflictions. Lines 22–30 offer a memorable myth of the birth of Ingratitude from the joining of Avarice and Suspicion, nursed by Envy, and thriving in the breasts of princes and kings. Immortal Ingratitude is personified as a quasi-Amazon brandishing three poisoned arrows (ll. 43–57)—one leaving favors received unreciprocated, one forgetting favors received, and one insulting benefactors of favors received. These mythical and symbolic allusions are reinforced by past and modern historical examples such as Scipio Africanus (ll. 73–129), Miltiades, Aristotle, Phocion (ll. 139–48), Julius Caesar (ll. 154–57), Ahmed Pasha (ll. 158–62), and Gonsalvo di Cordova (ll. 163–65), all destroyed by Ingratitude. Machiavelli ends these meditative tercets by admonishing all to ". . . flee from courts and governments, for there is no road that takes a man faster to weeping over what he longed for, when once he had gained it."[28]

The *Capitolo on Fortuna* (date unknown) is addressed to Giovanni Battista Soderini, brother of Piero Soderini, and a Florentine military leader. The *Capitolo* not only develops the ideas on *Fortuna* in *The Prince*, 25, but also reflects Dante's treatment of this theme in *Inferno* 7, 61–96. Several characteristics distinguish Machiavelli's originality. The lines show a remarkable facility to portray ideas utilizing metaphors, personification, analogies, and other figurative devices whose effect is visual, dramatic, and kinetic. This poetical essay is organized into distinct sections each contributing in its cumulative portrayal of *Fortuna*. Section I, ll. 1–45 defines the topic, announces the theme, states its didactic intention, and lists the qualities of this cruel goddess. Lines 46–63 describe the palace of this aged witch with two faces as containing numerous rotating wheels, each symbolizing a manner of aspiring to fame and wealth. The palace is populated by many occupants, each reacting physically, psychologically, and mentally to the rule of Fortune. Lines 100–26, a psychological analysis of man's nature as the basis for Fortune's overriding domination of his fate, are memorable not only for their perceptive insight, but also for the dynamic image of man as an

acrobat, leaping from one wheel to the next attempting to adjust
his character and behavior to Fortune's mutations. Lines 127–92
describe the narrative paintings which ornament the palace walls.
Although Machiavelli anticipates Ariosto's use of the device in *Orlando Furioso* 33, 1–58, he follows Virgil's epic precedent in *The
Aeneid*, I, when Aeneas sees the frescoes on the walls of Carthage
describing the Trojan war, and Dante in *Purgatory* X, ll. 28–105,
when the pilgrim sees the carved images of the great humilities.
The narrative paintings speak of the ascent and descent of great
ancient states, cities and leaders from Egypt to Rome, from Cyrus
and Alexander to Caesar and Pompey. Each image represents the
mutability of all things and the mutations of *Fortuna*. Two extended
similes mark this closing section. *Fortuna*'s shifting fury is compared
to the furious onrush of a rapid torrent destroying all in its path.
Later *Fortuna*'s cruel deception of man is compared to a rapacious
eagle who ". . . carries a tortoise on high, that the force of its fall
may break it, and he can feed on the dead flesh." Throughout this
allegorical parable Machiavelli suggests man's fragility before the
ineluctable uncertainties and vacillations of *Fortuna*—a view seemingly out of tune with the Renaissance humanist glorification of
man's power and ability to act. Man's only weapon in *Fortuna*'s game
is dramatized in the image of the agile, ever-moving wheel-dancer.
Stagnation and decline after success and glory can only be avoided
by following a dynamic conception of life which constantly adjusts
to the conditions.

The *Capitolo on Ambition* is dated by Gilbert as 1509 and by
Tusiani as 1516.[29] The similarity of the ideas and style to the Mantua
Legation letter of November 26, 1509, supports the first date, while
the reference to the fratricidal conflict of the Petrucci in Siena supports the second. Addressed to Luigi Guicciardini, brother of Francesco, the verse epistle first contemplates the origins, causes, and
examples of Ambition and then offers a corrective. The *Capitolo*
draws a realistic picture of the bloody, perverse effects of Ambition
in contemporary Italy. The ditches and streams are brimming with
bloody human bodies gashed and severed by Ambition. Originating
with man's fall and specifically with Cain, Ambition together with
Avarice have politically disrupted Italy and Tuscany. Only by dis-

cipline in the form of good laws—Judgment, Sound Intellect, Method, and Vigor—can man's egotistical appetite and envious nature be curbed and substituted with civic, military, and political *virtù*. Machiavelli's visual imagery is reinforced by the emotional, prophetic and apocalyptic tone pervading the poem as he calls on Italy and Florence to protect against Ambition hovering above readying for attack.

The *Capitolo on Chance* [Opportunity or Occasion] is a twenty-two line dialogue in *terza rima* modeled on Decimus Gallus Ausonius' *In Simulacrum Occasionis et Poenitentiae* [Epigram on the Statue of Occasion].[30] Opportunity describes herself to the poet as having one foot upon a wheel, wings on her feet, and disheveled hair which covers her face rendering her unrecognizable. The back of her head is bald preventing anyone from seizing her from behind or as she passes by. Penitence or Regret awaits he who loses Opportunity. The poem ends on a surprising note with Opportunity slipping from the poet's reach as they stood idly talking.

**Asino d' oro [*The Golden Ass*].** *The Golden Ass* (the original title was *L'asino*) probably dates to 1517.[31] Machiavelli mentions it in a letter to Lodovico Alamanni on December 17, 1517, complaining that Ariosto did not list Machiavelli in the *Orlando Furioso* among the notable poets of his age. The poem is an unfinished, *terza rima* satire on corrupt contemporary Florentine politics in which Machiavelli paradoxically imitates elements in Dante's *Comedy,* Apuleius' *Metamorphoses,* Plutarch's dialogues, Pliny's *Naturalis historia,* and book 10 of *The Odyssey.* The poem recounts how the speaker lost in a dark forest encounters an enchanting lady, one of Circe's assistants, who escorts him to her home. There he sees men transformed into beasts in accord with the kind of animal behavior they displayed in their political lives while in human form. Unlike the real animals of the natural world who live in harmony with their natures, each man-animal displays a defect which symbolizes the necessity to correct natural human inadequacies through controlled passions, rational contemplation, and political discipline. Following a banquet and an amorous interlude, the speaker, now left temporarily alone, meditates on the cause for the rise and fall of great states, on the cyclical-deterministic theory of history, on *Fortuna,*

and on the problem of liberty versus responsibility, among other
"Machiavellian" topics (ch. 5). Such meditation exposes man's
avarice, ambition, ingratitude and moral degeneration. The many
animals appearing in chs. 6 and 7 probably referred to Florentine
personalities Machiavelli had in mind; however, the poem breaks
off in ch. 8 at the point when the speaker is about to be turned into
an ass, and possibly by means of the "ass's bite" we might have been
informed of their identity. The poem is replete with Dantean allusions and it probably influenced Giovanni Battista Gelli's *Circe*
(1549), which in turn influenced Swift's "A Voyage to the
Houyhnhnms."[32]

*Carnival Songs* and other Occasional Poems. Machiavelli
composed six *Canti carnascialeschi* [Carnival Songs] based on a popular
Florentine genre of light, comic, and sometimes bawdy implications:
*De' diavoli iscacciati di cielo* [*Devils Driven Out From Heaven*, 1514;]
*Di amanti e donne disperati* [*Desperate Lovers and Ladies*, 1514]; *Degli
spiriti beati* [*The Blessed Spirits*, 1521]; *De' romiti*, [*The Hermits*, 1524];
*Di uomini che vendono le pine* [*Pine-Cone Vendors* 1524]; *De' ciurmadori*
[*Snake Charmers*]. The *Carnival Songs* explore amorous, patriotic, and
humorous topics. He also composed four sonnets, one quite early
to his father Messer Bernardo, and three to Giuliamo de' Medici,
following his removal from office. Finally, he wrote several innocuous
poems: *Serenade, Capitolo pastorale* [Pastoral Chapter], *Song, Strambotti,
Epigrams*, and two short poems to Barbara Salutari.

## Belfagor: *The Devil Who Married*

*Belfagor* (date unknown) is the short novella of how Pluto, the
wise, just ruler of the Infernal region, sends his archfiend, named
Belfagor, to earth at the advice of his counsellors to investigate the
numerous complaints of those in hell that it was through their wives
that they suffer perdition. Belfagor, in human form arrives on earth
with 100,000 ducats, chooses Florence as his home since it was
reknowned for its usury. There he selects the name Roderigo of
Castile, rents a house on the Street of All Saints, and marries Onesta,
the beautiful daughter of Amerigo Donati, an important, respected
Florentine. Roderigo falls in love with his wife and indulges her

every whim. With each indulgence she becomes more petulant, vain, proud, and extravagant until she dominates him and exhausts his money. Roderigo's creditors declare him bankrupt, but he succeeds in avoiding imprisonment by fleeing his wife and the city. During his escape he is harbored by Gianmatteo del Brica, a farmer, who hides Roderigo in a dungheap. In gratitude, Roderigo confers on Gianmatteo the power, and attendant financial rewards, of exorcizing devils, assuring him that the devil he exorcizes would be he, Roderigo-Belfagor. Soon enough Gianmatteo learns that a young Florentine woman is possessed by a demon. He succeeds in his exorcism and is well remunerated. King Charles of Naples, after hearing of Gianmatteo's skill, asks him to perform the same miracle on his possessed daughter. Roderigo grants his assistance, but warns him that since he has met his obligation to the farmer for saving his life he will no longer help him. Gianmatteo accepts Roderigo's decision and returns to Florence rich. King Louis VII of France learns of Gianmatteo's power and the farmer is reluctantly sent to assist the King in the exorcism of his daughter. At the prospect of more wealth, Gianmatteo once again asks Roderigo's assistance, but is violently rebuffed. Intent on having his way, Gianmatteo devises a plan to outwit the devil. A large wooden platform is erected in the square of Notre Dame with an altar set in the middle and a group of twenty musicians on one side. When Gianmatteo lifts his hand during the ceremony the band is to commence playing as loudly as possible and rush to the altar. The ceremony begins and Roderigo is ready to impose his revenge on the disobedient farmer when suddenly at Gianmatteo's signal the band strikes up its noisy clamor. Roderigo is shocked and asks what it is all about. Gianmatteo informs him it is his wife coming to get him. Terrified, Roderigo flees to peaceful, well-ordered hell where he confirms the complaints against wives, and Gianmatteo, outwitting the devil, lives happily ever after.

Although the story presents the misogynistic and anti-matrimonial theme of the exploitative wife too terrible even for the devil, the satire seems more directed at the superstitions and corrupted customs of the credulous Florentines. Through the use of ironic inversion Machiavelli exposes religious hypocrisy, fear, and political

ineptitude. Pluto is more wise than the earthly kings, the devil
Belfagor is not so deceitful and diabolical as Gianmatteo, and hell
is a much better place to live than earth.

## Chapter Seven
# The Legacy of Machiavelli

The study of Machiavelli's impact on subsequent generations presents a disorienting task perhaps more challenging than the study of his works.[1] Each generation has been impelled to respond to Machiavelli's meaning and possible application. He has been viewed as a spokesman of tyranny and immorality, the founder of modern political science, and the father of nationalism. For many he is the supreme interpreter of Renaissance political theory and practice. The many facets of "Machiavellism" have been treated in hundreds of books and articles, attesting to the continued fascination with his political theories, historical vision, and psychological perceptions. The vastness of this aspect of Machiavelli studies permits only a cursory bibliographic synthesis. The Machiavelli legacy extends beyond sixteenth century Florence and Italy to affect various national cultures as perhaps no other writer has. Not intended to duplicate the extensive work of others in this area, the purpose of this brief survey of Machiavelli's living legacy is (1) to provide an introductory bibliographic overview of his fortunes which might facilitate deeper study of a subject treated by specialists; (2) to indicate a few of the high points in the history of Machiavellism which have enlarged, enriched, and distorted the dimensions of the original legacy; (3) to synthesize the major trends in the evolution of Machiavellism within national boundaries. Emphasis will be placed on the early stages of this evolution when many of the trends were established, since a clear picture of these earlier phases is essential to subsequent developments.

### Definitions of Machiavellism

The terms "Machiavellism," "Machiavellian," "Anti-Machiavellism," "neo-Machiavellism," are conventionalized epithets describing some aspect of the Florentine's life or writings. Frequently deriving their reference from a simplistic reading of *The Prince,* "Machiavellism" and "Machiavellian" pejoratively denote cunning, cruel, hypocritical, unscrupulous, immoral, and deceitful political behavior. Machiavelli's name so used means underhanded, tortuous, intriguing behavior practiced by an atheistic, diabolical opportunist with a potential for homicide. His violent and treacherous character is often encapsulated in the animal symbols of the lion and the fox. Conjoined with the meaning that Machiavellism describes the actions of the despotic tyrant, who rationalizes his acts with claims of benefiting the welfare of the state, is the implication added later that it describes the violent or dissembling behavior of any person intent on personal ambition and gain. Such a connotation suggests a superman, autonomous and self-directed. Another implication is that Machiavelli himself provided the model for behavior which exploits human frailties, victimizes the weak, naive, or trusting, and manipulates events through force or trickery. Without basis in verified biographical fact, and often divorced from direct knowledge of his works and their historical milieu, the most frequent current use of the term "Machiavellian" denotes scheming, serpentine behavior finding its origins in Machiavelli's personal character as though he had been its inventor.[2] Thus, he is transformed into an insidious beguiler, an incarnation of immorality, an infamous, abominable disciple of Satan counseling acts of fraud, duplicity, and every other kind of dishonesty.

Yet "Machiavellism" and "Machiavellian" have acquired meanings exceeding these popular, misconceived dimensions particularly among those who have studied the reputation and influence of Machiavelli's works. In this context the terms are associated with the progressive fortune of his writings and the polemic which they have inspired. Such a study presupposes a thorough, firsthand knowledge of his biography, writings, and historical milieu, and it includes a comparative examination of the various editions and translations of his writings over the years. It deals with (1) how his ideas have been diffused, interpreted, exploited, distorted, applied, and rationalized; (2) what aspects of his thought, method, and style have operated as inspirational catalysts; (3) what innovative, revolutionary contributions Machiavelli made which prompted further analysis and resulted in the advancement of knowledge; and (4) what effects his works have had in the everyday world of events. Such a systematic study may include a rejection for whatever reason of the legitimacy of his theories, vision, and methodology—a rejection often termed "anti-Machiavellian,"[3]—or an acceptance of their universality and authenticity—currently referred to as "neo-Machiavellian."

## The Origins of Machiavellism and Anti-Machiavellism

Although Machiavelli's life reflected few of the qualities associated with the pejorative epithets derived from his name, biographical data provided the substructure for the future engrossment of the satanic legend. During his diplomatic career some grew to dislike Machiavelli because of his association with the Soderini government, as was evident in Biagio Buonaccorsi's 1502 warning that Machiavelli show more prudence in his dealings with the political opposition. His major modern biographers, Tommasini, Villari, Prezzolini, and Ridolfi, suggest how aspects of his character exposed to the not-so-well-meaning interpreters paved the way for the preposterous judgments about his life and writings.

Italy was regarded as a place of intrigue and iniquity and Machiavelli as an Italian was identified with the stereotypes persisting in foreign circles. As a Florentine he attracted the prejudice of non-Italians and non-Florentines, not to say the curious self-condemnation Florentines enjoyed dispensing on their compatriots. To most, Machiavelli's intelligence, perception, and resoluteness was undercut by his witty, cynical, and detached manner. He boasted of vices which from available evidence he did not possess, and hid his virtues—his cheerful, sensitive, generous, and passionate nature—behind a mask of sarcasm, self-dramatization, and self-derision. The physical traits revealed in Santi di Tito's portrait, probably derived from a death mask, reinforced these superficial impressions and promoted the legend, particularly the penetrating dark eyes, the subtle compressed lips turned slightly in a half-ironical smile as though savoring some private joke at the observer's expense, and the high, prominent, feline cheeks.[4]

The unpredictability of Florentine politics toward the end of Machiavelli's life and immediately after his death contributed to these semibiographical origins of the legend. After his death, *The Prince* appeared in print in 1532 just two years after the fall of another republican government in Florence and the reinstatement of the Medici with Alessandro, the illegitimate son of Lorenzo, Duke of Urbino. The constitutional changes he implemented combined with the work on the Fortezza da Basso, viewed by many as a tyrannical symbol of princely power, and the exile of Florentine republicans such as G. B. Busini (1504–1574?), conspired against a neutral evaluation of Machiavelli's works.[5] Busini's 1549 letter to Varchi (1503–1565) recounting Machiavelli's return to Florence in May 1527 just before his death, outlines both the hostility of republican exiles, who felt Machiavelli had betrayed their cause, and sketches the future dimensions of the Machiavelli myth: his desperate attempts to regain favor and political employment at any ideological cost, the ambivalent, uninformed interpretations of *The Prince,* motivated by political, economic, and religious self-interest, the personal vituperation and character assassination.[6]

The origins of Machiavellism and anti-Machiavellism can also be traced to the complicated intermingling of religious, political, and philosophical forces in the second half of the sixteenth century. Once *The Prince* left the intimate, accepting circle of Machiavelli's friends and colleagues, who were in no way scandalized by the work, it provoked posthumous controversy in the Papacy. The Church, attempting to retain its threatened temporal power and reinforce its questioned spiritual dogmatism, violently opposed any suggestion of a secular, self-justifying state *(raison d'état)* independent of Church authority. It opposed the "Machiavellian" idea that politics was a secular, autonomous activity, religion a political instrument, and man's political conduct exempted from reference to God.[7] Even though *The Prince* had originally appeared with Pope Clement VII's imprimatur, in 1559 Pope Paul IV placed it on the Index, where it remained until 1890. In 1562 the Council of Trent confirmed his papal edict. Catholic opposition spread, skillfully voiced often through the Jesuits, who ironically were accused by Protestants, anti-Papists, and others of utilizing Machiavellian methods.[8] The

Reformation and the Counterreformation presented additional fronts for the Machiavellism controversy, finding its greatest battleground in the French Huguenot opposition to Catherine de' Medici whom they blamed for the St. Bartholomew's massacre. Catherine and her Italian counselors were viewed as foreign *Machiavélistes*, immoral, libertine atheists seeking to impose tyrannical rule. Huguenot opposition, as epitomized by its supreme exponent, Innocent Gentillet, was similar to Italian Catholic opposition to what was thought to be the major repercussions of Machiavellian thought—a naturalistic conception of the state.[9]

## Italy's Contribution to the Machiavelli Legacy

In his December 10, 1513, letter to Vettori about the composition of *The Prince,* Machiavelli envisioned that someone would plagiarize his work. In speculating on whether he should present *The Prince* in person to Giuliano, Machiavelli expressed his fear that in not doing so Piero Ardinghelli, secretary to Pope Leo X and Medici confidant, would usurp his ideas and offer them to his patrons as original. Instead, some ten years later, on March 26, 1523, Agostino Nifo da Sessa (1474–1538 or 1545), a professor at Pisa, published a Latin work entitled *De regnandi peritia ad Carolum V imperatorem,* a blatant plagiarism of Machiavelli's masterpiece.[10] With Nifo begins the tradition of the exploitative use of Machiavelli's works, the distortion of his ideas, the neglect of the interrelationship of his political purposes, thought, and rhetorical strategies. As early as the May 8, 1532, edition of *The Prince,* the publisher, Bernardo Giunta, acknowledged the Latin plagiarism in the preface. Blado's preface to the 1531 edition of the *Discourses* also complained of the illegal appropriation of Machiavelli's works.[11]

The earliest Florentine reactions to Machiavelli's work before and after his death were generally positive and admiring, as, for example, those of Vettori, Buondelmonti, Cardinal Salviati, Buonaccorsi, and others.[12] Donato Giannotti, Machiavelli's chancery successor, reflects in his two major works, *Della repubblica fiorentina* and his 1528 militia proposal, a perceptive understanding of Machiavelli's ideas and purposes and an assimilation of his style and approach.[13] Machiavelli's most astute contemporary critic was Francesco Guicciardini with whom Machiavelli corresponded after their first meeting in 1521 until his death. Guicciardini's *Considerations on the "Discourses" of Machiavelli* (1530) represents the first attempt to combine a history of Machiavelli's fortune with a history of the criticism he inspired.[14] Although they differed in personality, class awareness, method, attitude toward history, political and religious ideologies, and vision of human nature, the thought-provoking, controversial nature of Machiavelli's writings stimulated Guicciardini's best work. Other early Florentine historians, such as Segni (1504–1558), Nardi (1476–1563), and Varchi, contributed to the extension of the Machiavelli legend by often praising his genius, but deploring his unscrupulousness, ideas formulated early in Busini's letter to Varchi. Giovio's (1483–1552) early biographical sketch of Machiavelli also resorted to dualistic praise and condemnation. Moreover, Machiavelli's plays became the source book for literary writers, such as G. M. Cecchi (1518–1587), Doni (1513–1574), Gelli (1498–1563), among others, and admiring Tuscan writers, inhibited by Church condemnation of Machiavelli, attempted to save the works of their fellow Florentine by purging them of what was objectionable.[15] Finally, outside Florence, Machiavelli inspired dozens of responses, signalling the hundreds he would provoke in subsequent centuries.[16]

While in the sixteenth century Machiavelli became the battleground for the conflict between the theocratic state and the emerging national-secular monarchy, many seventeenth-century treatises focused on a compromise between the concept of divine right and the idea of *raison d'état*. They noted Machiavelli's emphasis on political realism and the usefulness of history's lessons. The eighteenth century reevaluated Machiavelli as part of its general reassessment of politics viewed not so much as an expedient for the acquisition and preservation of power, but rather as an instrument to alter the course of history and reinstate man's natural rights. Machiavelli was justified as a product of the intrigue and violence of his time, and his importance was related to the political situation of eighteenth-century Italy in which politics operated both as an instrument of tyranny and liberty. The eighteenth century, through such patriotic writers as Alfieri, Parini, Algarotti, among others inspired by nationalistic idealism, transmitted to the nineteenth century the image of a republican Machiavelli, a prophet of Italian unity, the savior who for the first time envisioned and promoted Italy as an organic and independent political entity—*la patria*—distinct from the *nazioni barbariche* that had for centuries occupied, exploited, and destroyed its resources and culture. Even a philosopher such as Giambattista Vico, who proceeded from religious presuppositions inconsistent with *The Prince*, nevertheless, reflected Machiavelli's continued influence. Vico's metaphysical view of ideal, eternal history builds on Machiavelli's experience and reflections. Vico extended Machiavelli's idea of the autonomous state as the agent by which a people's history is fulfilled through its birth, development, and progressive transformation.[17]

The nineteenth century, through historians such as V. Cuoco, in his *Viaggio in Italia nel secolo di Leone decimo* (1804), reinforced the historical approach to Machiavelli. In the Catholic orientation of such historians as Cesare Cantù, Cesare Balbo, Giuseppe Mazzini, Gino Capponi, and others, evidence of the dualistic opinion coexisted—praise, for his patriotism and his prose style, and hostility for his immorality. Ugo Foscolo's (1778–1827) admiration for Machiavelli is seen in his work, *Last Letters of Jacopo Ortis* (1802), in which Jacopo's negative attitude resembles Machiavelli's so-called deterministic pessimism. Ortis shares Machiavelli's love for Italy and his disillusionment at witnessing his nation's self-destructive divisiveness and provincialism. In Foscolo's poem, *Of Tombs* (1806), this admiration passionately culminates. Foscolo identifies with the earlier views of Rousseau and Alfieri, who affirmed the oblique intention of *The Prince*, seeing Machiavelli as the champion of the people while pretending to counsel tyranny. In the political-critical commentary, *On the Country, Life, Writings and Fame of N. Machiavelli* (1811), Foscolo rejects the anti-Machiavellian literature, painting the Florentine as a loyal patriot forced by political circumstances to advocate unscrupulousness. Foscolo undoubtedly occupies an important place in the history of the Machiavelli legacy and objectifies the revision of critical opinion which typified the Romantic period.[18]

Francesco De Sanctis culminates nineteenth-century Italy's historical renewal of Machiavelli's legacy. In his mammoth *Storia della letteratura italiana*, De Sanctis portrays Machiavelli both as the epitome of the Renaissance spirit and the first example of modern man. Machiavelli's unclouded perception, honest irreverence, and knowing irony are viewed as a rejection of the forms and mentality of the Middle Ages and the sloth and aesthetic evasion of the Renaissance. De Sanctis sees Machiavelli as the scrutinizing critic of the past and present and the precursor of the future. His compact reconstruction of Machiavelli's basic theories is a creative reinterpretation of the relationships between Machiavelli and his times. He is recognized both as a man of his age and as a perennial contemporary with universal meaning. With De Sanctis initiates the idea, to become more prevalent with modern scholars, that a true understanding of Machiavelli means an enlightened recognition of his profound morality.[19]

Nineteenth-century historicism developed a remarkable group of Machiavelli biographers and literary analysts who transmitted his legacy to the twentieth century. Villari's *Niccolò Machiavelli e i suoi tempi* and Tommasini's *La vita e gli scritti di N. M. nella loro relazione col machiavellismo* are classic studies of his private and public life, of the genesis and content of his works, of the total context in which he wrote. Yet the comprehensiveness characterizing these works accounts for their basic flaws, particularly the unrelated digressions, inexact dating, wordy and unfocused discussions.[20] The nineteenth century is notable for (1) its historical approach, (2) its discovery and vindication of Machiavelli's nationalism, (3) its recognition of the interrelationship of Machiavelli's works, and particularly the reconciliation between *The Prince* and the *Discourses*.

In the twentieth century Benedetto Croce established the idea, which found its origins in the sixteenth-century politicoreligious controversy surrounding Machiavelli, that the Florentine had discovered pure politics and systematized the autonomy of politics from morality. When Croce looked at Machiavelli some twenty-four years after his *Machiavelli e Vico,* he turned his attention in *Una questione che forse non si chiuderà mai: la questione del Machiavelli* (Bari, 1949) to a critique of what he believed was Machiavelli's failure to reconcile politics and morality. Croce emphasized too much the supposed distinctions in Machiavelli between individual politics and universal morality.[21] The Fascist period contributed Francesco Ercole (*La po-*

*litica di Machiavelli*, Rome, 1926), who analyzed Machiavelli's terminology, transforming him into a theoretician and utilizing him to justify the Fascist state. Machiavelli has also attracted Italian Marxists, as exemplified in Gramsci's vision of *The Prince* as a revolutionary document.[22]

## The Early French Travesty of Machiavelli

Machiavelli's works were well known in France through translations of *The Prince* (1553), of the first book of the *Discourses* (1544) and of *The Art of War* (1546). There is no suggestion in these French translations, or in the comments by Guillaume Capel or Jacques Gohory, Machiavelli's early translators, of the anti-Machiavellian motifs Innocent Gentillet would popularize in 1576 with his *Discours sur les moyens de bien gouverner et maintenir en paix un royaume, ou autre principauté. Contre Nicholas Machiavel florentin*. The work was written first in French, dedicated to the Duke François Alençon, and then translated into Latin and various other languages.[23] Gentillet was a member of the Huguenot sect, a Protestant minority consistently opposed to the localization of power in a monarchy, particularly one with perverse Italian origins which threatened French national identity. Catherine de' Medici had hoped to eliminate the opposing pressures of Catholics and Protestants by allowing the 1572 St. Bartholomew massacre. Catherine, as an Italian, a Florentine and a Medici (the family to whom Machiavelli had addressed *The Prince*), was viewed as the instrument of Machiavelli's tyrannical theories. Thus, contemporary historical events were attributed to Machiavelli's ideas and their application by Catherine who, it was claimed, had substituted the Bible with *The Prince*. The French Protestants viewed Machiavellism as another more sinister face of corrupt Roman papism and intolerant Jesuitism. Ironically, in the Catholic Countermovement the Jesuits condemned Machiavelli as an accomplice in the Reformation. Through this secondhand distortion Gentillet attempted to reaffirm national pride, expunge foreign influence, protect the dwindling rights of the French nobility of which he was a part, and assert the religious rights of a minority.[24]

The historical importance of Gentillet's work resides in how, through its wide diffusion in various translations outside of France and particularly in England, it became the sourcebook for many commonplace myths about Machiavelli. Especially influential was the 1577 Latin translation to which the anonymous translator attached an Epistle dedicatory which along with the original work was translated. Simon Patericke's 1602 English translation of Gentillet's French original includes a translation of the Latin Epistle dedicatory. It was through this Latin translation with its Epistle dedicatory that the Calvinists identified Machiavelli with Satan's war against the Gospels.[25] Machiavelli inspired a few defenses, like that by the Florentine resident in France, Paolo Mini (*Difesa della città di Firenze et dei Fiorentini contro le calunnie et maldicentie de' maligni,* Lyon, 1577) and that in the next century by Gabriele Naudé (*Considérations politiques sur les coups d'état,* Rome, 1639); however, Duplessis Mornay's *Vendiciae contra tyrannos* (Basel, 1589) exemplifies the exploitative, closet use of Machiavelli—public condemnation, but often private plagiarism or hidden approbation.

The work of Jean Bodin (1530–1596) represents, after Gentillet's subjective manipulation, an important contribution in the illumination of the Florentine's legacy. Bodin's two major writings, *Methodus ad facilem historiarum cognitionem* (1566) and the *Six livres de la République* (1576), show not only firsthand knowledge of Machiavelli, but also how his thought could generate its contradiction, anti-Machiavellism, while forming the basis for continued positive exploration of the questions he raised. Bodin was a member of the *Politiques* party, advocate of the *raison d'état,* intent on freeing the state from Church power and secular factionalism. Bodin is recognized for the juridical character of his argument, for establishing, if not discovering, the legal features of the State's national authority and sovereignty vested in the crown. Bodin, aware of the problem of reconciling the *Prince* with the *Discourses,* was perhaps the first to discern the interrelationship of Machiavelli's political vision and historical theories, an important advance in comprehending the implications of his legacy and an object of considerable future study.

The defamatory campaign initiated by the French Calvinists had a long tradition in France during the seventeenth and eighteenth centuries, one which contributed little in understanding Machiavelli's thought and method, and much in advancing the myths. A typical instance is the questionably motivated diatribe, *Antimachiavel* (1740), Voltaire wrote for Frederick of Prussia. In the nineteenth century, however, the literary histories of Ginguemé (*Histoire littéraire d' Italie*, 1811–19) and Sismondi (*Littérature du midi de l'Europe*, 1813) reaffirmed Machiavelli's republican views, emphasized the circuitous intention of *The Prince*, and proclaimed the historical and literary importance of his prose style, all part of the Romantic rehabilitation of Machiavelli.[26]

## The English Machiavel

The Satanic myth which took root in France thrived in England where the political and religious controversy against Machiavelli became more explicit, inspired by and connected with, historical figures and events and unaccompanied by a dispassionate study of the works. After his death Machiavelli's biography and works assumed a second life. The outward condemnation and private application in Italy and France reflecting the coexistence of repulsion and admiration, seemed greater in England than anywhere else. The black legend of "Old Nick" as the prototype of nefariousness and criminality gained immense proportions because as nowhere else the political and religious controversy was translated into literary, dramatic terms. The flourishing literature of Renaissance England operated as the transmitting vehicle by which "Machiavellian politics" was popularized. Some serious thinkers showed a genuine interest in Machiavelli's ideas. They saw that the lessons in his works represented a stark modification of traditional concepts and points of view, a revised conception of political relationships and realities that could foster more resolute and efficacious results. Influential Italians residing in England, such as Alberico Gentili, an Oxford law professor (1552–1608), attempted, through an oblique interpretation of Machiavelli's satiric intention, to correct misconceptions (*De Legationibus*, London, 1585).

Although France played a significant role in carrying the Machiavelli legend from Italy across the channel to England, the earlier view that it was primarily through Gentillet's work as translated by Simon Patericke that the English knew of Machiavelli has now been refuted.[27] Machiavelli was available to the English before Gentillet both in manuscript and printed form, in Italian, Latin, and English. Authorized and illicit printed Italian editions done by the London printer, John Wolfe, appeared with false imprints in the 1580s, *The Prince* and *Discourses* in 1584, *The Art of War* (no date), *The History of Florence* in 1587, and *The Golden Ass* in 1588. Although the Dacres printed translations of *The Prince* and the *Discourses* did not appear until 1636 and 1640, Peter Whitehorne dedicated his 1563, 1573, and 1588 English translations of *The Art of War* to Queen Elizabeth, and Thomas Bedingfield's translations of *The History of Florence* appeared in 1595. Seven manuscripts of *The Prince*, representing three distinct English translations, and three manuscripts of the *Discourses,* two incomplete, have been uncovered as well. A 1553 French translation done by Guillaume Capel and dedicated to James Hamilton, second Earl of Arran, has been discovered. Obviously, the well-traveled English also picked up the readily available Latin and Italian editions.[28] That Gentillet was not the exclusive source of Elizabethan misunderstanding about Machiavelli is also supported by the existence of a number of pre-Gentillet allusions to Machiavelli particularly in private correspondence where there was less reticence to discuss his ideas and even traces of reluctant confirmation.[29] Recently critics have placed more importance on the 1577 Latin translation of Gentillet with its Epistle dedicatory than on the French original or the 1602 Patericke English translation for diffusion of Gentillet's travesty in England. Patericke's Epistle faithfully translates the one prefaced to the Latin edition of Gentillet. The Latin translator, probably T. Beza or Lambert Daneau, dedicated the work to the Englishmen F. Hastings and E. Bacon with the intention of making Gentillet known outside of France, and in 1602 Patericke translated the Latin Epistle leaving the date and dedicatees intact.[30]

Perhaps the first vehement English denouncer of Machiavelli was Cardinal Reginald Pole (1500–1558), whose conflict with Henry VIII about the relationship between Church authority and the king's power became the catalyst for the *Apologia ad Carolum Quintum* (between 1535 and 1545). Pole identified with the aristocracy in the struggle for power between the Tudor monarchy and the lords. He opposed Henry's defiance of Church authority, a defiance Pole believed was counseled by the king's advisor Thomas Cromwell. Supposedly, in 1528 Pole had an interview with Cromwell to discuss the Cardinal's opposition and his attempt to subjugate the English monarchy to papal authority. As they discussed the qualities and responsibilities of a king's counsellors, Cromwell is purported to have alluded to *The Prince,* suggesting to Pole that his naive, impractical, and unrealistic political views might be corrected by a reading of this book. It would seem Pole followed Cromwell's suggestion. *The Prince* inspired his condemnation in the *Apologia* and his accusation that as the Satanic counselor of tyrants Machiavelli had caused the Anglican schism by providing Cromwell with a sourcebook of perverse political devices intended to consolidate secular power devoid of spiritual values and goals.[31] The *Apologia* reveals, however, Pole's firsthand knowledge of *The Prince,* if not full awareness of its place in the Machiavelli canon.

The Machiavelli polemic provided new literary and dramatic material. The study of how English dramatists used the Machiavelli controversy offers insight into the complex, many-sided, and paradoxical sixteenth-century English response to his work. Modern scholarship has revised most of the traditional conclusions about Machiavelli's reputation and impact in Tudor England. The fascination with heroes who reflected the evil of Machiavelli's view of human nature may suggest an ambivalent psychological attraction for the superman genius and repulsion at the tyrannical equivocator. Yet the stage Machiavel, as epitomized in such characters as Barabas *(The Jew of Malta),* Bosola *(The Duchess of Malfi),* Iago, Lorenzo *(The Spanish Tragedy),* Mendoza *(Malcontent),* Richard III, Edmund *(Lear),* Flamineo *(White Devil),* and others, synthesizes several literary traditions, among them the medieval morality Vice figure, the conventional portrayal of Lucifer in Miracle plays, and the Senecan stock villain. In surveying how the theoretical discussions of Machiavelli became popularized in the stage Machiavel, it is clear that (1) sixteenth-century England reflected a wide range of irreconcilable attitudes from admiration to condemnation, (2) Gentillet was not the primary vehicle for English knowledge of Machiavelli, and (3) the English response was determined not by a sympathetic understanding of how his work reflected contemporary Italian and

Florentine history and politics, but rather how the English related his ideas to their possible application in their own national context.[32]

Transmission of Machiavellism occurred through less popular and more philosophical writing as well as seen in Francis Bacon's (1561–1626) generally positive evaluation. Bacon, however, was not so concerned with Italian politics and history as he was with Machiavelli's secular, utilitarian validity in practical life and his application to English problems. Bacon defended Machiavelli both in terms of theoretical and practical morality. Bacon applauded the efficaciousness of the inductive and empirical methodology he saw reflected in the *Discourses*. He was one of the first to view Machiavelli's use of idealized historical example as a curriculum of moral education for effective action in practical living. There are several revealing references in Bacon's major works (*Advancement of Learning* [1605], *De Augmentis Scientiarum* [1623], *Essays*—[1625]) and traces of Machiavelli's influence in his minor works.[33] Bacon seems to have understood the rhetorical design behind Machiavelli's idealized historical types. His reaction represents a significant advance in the history and meaning of "Machiavellism" and in his application to areas outside politics and history, a practice which would extend Machiavelli's original legacy perhaps farther than any could imagine. Just as the reform motive inspired Machiavelli's ideas on the relationship between politics and history, Bacon was likewise a reformer in philosophy and science. Both, although accused of irreligiousness, nevertheless, saw the role that religion must and could play in advancing their respective reform proposals.[34]

The utopian element Bacon perceived as an educational and moral force in Machiavelli also associates him to Thomas More's (1478–1535) *Utopia,* written in 1516 when Machiavelli dedicated his final version of *The Prince* to Lorenzo. Although the two wrote independently without being mutually influenced, their relationship resides in their reformative goals, in the tension between realist and moralist pervading their work, and in their utopian tendencies.[35] More certain is Machiavelli's influence on Sir Philip Sidney's *Arcadia,* on its moral and political ideas and on the Machiavel villains who reinforce the identity of their political ideologies.[36] The historical view which Sir Walter Raleigh (1552?–1618) expounds in his ambitious work *The*

*History of the World* reflects Raleigh's familiarity with *The Prince,* the *Discourses,* and *The History of Florence.* Although Raleigh seems to criticize Machiavelli in his less important *Maxims of State,* the Machiavellian influence is profound and fundamental. Raleigh, like More and Sidney, relates to Machiavelli in how he demonstrates the Renaissance tension between a worldly and a theological approach to politics and history.[37] Evidence of Machiavelli's impact can be found in Edmund Spenser's (1552–1599) *Mother Hubberd's Tale* (1591) and *View of the Present State of Ireland* (1596), in John Donne's *Ignatius his Conclave* (1611) as well as in Hobbes, Harrington, Milton, Hume, Neville, Bolingbroke. The English Renaissance assimilated the Machiavellism trends set in Italy and France and contributed its own dimensions to the original legacy. Although the politics of integrity was probably advocated, a double standard permeated the English response which often indiscriminately blended in ideas apparently similar to but not identical with Machiavelli's. Undoubtedly, Machiavellism, perhaps more than any other continental phenomenon with the possible exception of Petrarchanism, profoundly influenced English Renaissance culture, continuing to do so into the eighteenth and nineteenth centuries. The Romantic poets, among them Wordsworth, Coleridge, Southey, Landor, Byron, Shelley, reflect admiration, culminating in Lord Macauley's serious historical reevaluation.[38] Although every European nation possesses a history of national Machiavellism,[39] England's contribution to this phenomenon is perhaps the richest and most far-reaching.

## The Modern Machiavelli

The Machiavelli legacy undergoes reevaluation today not only in political and historical thought but in seemingly irrelevant disciplines. Critics have discovered a new value to *The Prince*'s final exhortative chapter in terms of how its identification of freedom with the need to export war applies today.[40] Some argue that western world-leaders under the threat of Communism should implement Machiavelli's power principles free of limiting moralistic concerns.[41] Others have compared Italy and Florence of the 1500s with today's developing nations to show the immediacy of his ideas on leadership to the contemporary nation builder.[42] The humanistic dimensions of his theories have impressed those concerned with the modern technological and scientific emphasis.[43] His impact on United States history, constitutional development, and political thought has come under close study recently.[44] Educators perceive the pedagogical relevance of his ideas on leadership and diplomacy to the classroom teacher.[45] Psychologists have used Machiavelli to construct personality instruments measuring manipulative orientation, while the science of management explores his relevance to the politics of corporate life.[46] The popular interest in Machiavelli was reflected in a supplement to the *New York Review of Books* which surveyed his works, outlined approaches, and speculated on modern application.[47]

Anyone undertaking the study of Machiavelli is overwhelmed by the critical literature, particularly that of the twentieth century. The fragmentary, discursive nature of Machiavelli studies today indicates a real need for a comprehensive bibliography of twentieth-century scholarship. Norsa's Italian bibliography ends with 1935, uses a confusing inaccessible thematic organization, contains no annotations or citations of American scholarship, among other faults and inadequacies.[48] Although Fido's survey helps for the earlier centuries, the traditional literary focus on his approach ignores important studies in other disciplines especially in the last twenty-five years. Short surveys of twentieth-century advances exist,[49] yet the significance of Machiavelli's contemporary influence warrants a compendium which would (1) promote synthesis rather than fragmentism, (2) recognize his interdisciplinary appeal, and (3) suggest areas which require further exploration.[50] The analysis of his works in the preceding chapters of this book has taken into account noteworthy twentieth-century developments. This eclectic approach has considered generalized and biographical studies; research on manuscripts, dating, structure, and value; linguistic studies; literary, poetical, artistic approaches; novel interpretations of his ideas. The remarkable spectrum of contributions made by numerous national scholars, written in diverse languages, reflecting distinct perspectives and disciplines, justifies John Morley's claim that Machiavelli is indeed a "citizen of all countries."[51]

# Notes and References

## Chapter One

1. The most authoritative life is Roberto Ridolfi, *The Life of Niccolò Machiavelli*, trans. Cecil Grayson (Chicago, 1963). Classic biographies are Giuseppe Prezzolini, *Machiavelli*, trans. G. Savini (New York, 1967); Oreste Tommasini, *La vita e gli scritti di Niccolò Machiavelli*, 2 vols. (Rome, 1883–1911); Pasquale Villari, *The Life and Times of Niccolò Machiavelli*, trans. Linda Villari, 2 vols. (1892; rpt. New York, 1969). New interpretations are Charles D. Tarlton, *Fortune's Circle: A Biographical Interpretation of Niccolò Machiavelli* (Chicago, 1970); Edmond Barincou, *Machiavelli*, trans. Helen R. Lane (New York: Grove Press, 1961); J. R. Hale, *Machiavelli and Renaissance Italy* (London, 1961).

2. Villari, *Life*, I, 219; Prezzolini, *Machiavelli*, p. 8; Luigi Firpo, "La vita," *Terzo Programma* 10 (1970):15–22.

3. Bernardo Machiavelli, *Libro di Ricordi*, ed. C. Olschki (Florence: Olschki, 1954).

4. Ibid., *Libro*, p. 103.

5. Ridolfi, *Life*, p. 257.

6. B. Machiavelli, *Libro*, p. 222.

7. Prezzolini, *Machiavelli*, p. 27.

8. Domenico Maffei, *Il giovane Machiavelli: Banchiere con Berto Berti a Roma* (Florence: Giunti, G. Barbera, for the Banca Toscana, 1973).

9. On the Medici in the fifteenth to sixteenth centuries, see in addition to Machiavelli's *History of Florence*, Francesco Guicciardini, *The History of Florence*, trans. Mario Domandi (New York: Harper & Row, 1970); Vespasiano, *Renaissance Princes, Popes, and Prelates. The Vespasiano Memoirs: Lives of Illustrious Men of the XVth Century*, trans. William George and Emily Waters (New York: Harper & Row, 1963); Ferdinand Schevill, *The Medici* (New York: Harper & Row, 1949); J. H. Whitfield, Machiavelli (New York, 1965); Sara Sturm, *Lorenzo de' Medici* (New York: Twayne, 1974); Christopher Hibbert, *The House of Medici: Its Rise and Fall* (New York: Morrow, 1975).

10. *The Chief Works and Others*, trans. Allan H. Gilbert III (Durham, 1965), p. 1435.

11. Nicolai Rubinstein, "Politics and Constitution in Florence at the
End of the Fifteenth Century," in *Italian Renaissance Studies,* ed. E. F. Jacob
(London: Faber & Faber, 1960), p. 182.

12. Whitfield, *Machiavelli,* p. 25, says, based on Landucci's diary, that
15,000 attended Savonarola's sermons daily.

13. Guicciardini, *History of Florence,* pp. 97–117; Villari, *Life,* I,
203–14; R. Ridolfi, *The Life of Girolamo Savonarola* (London: Routledge
& Kegan Paul, 1959).

14. Gennaro Sasso, *Niccolò Machiavelli: Storia del suo pensiero politico*
(Naples, 1958), p. 9; Rubinstein, "Politics and Constitution in Florence,"
p. 182.

15. Guicciardini, *History of Florence,* p. 126.

16. Villari, *Life,* I, 212; Guicciardini, *History of Florence,* pp. 138–45.

17. *The Letters of Machiavelli,* trans. Allan Gilbert (New York, 1961),
pp. 86–88; *Lettere,* ed. Franco Gaeta (Milan, 1961), pp. 29–31. The
analysis of Machiavelli's writings takes into account the Italian text.

18. Gilbert inserts quotes, while Gaeta does not.

19. Sasso, *Storia,* pp. 15–16.

20. Luigi Russo, *Machiavelli,* 4th ed. (Bari, 1974), pp. 13–18.

21. E. H. Harbison, *The Intellectual as Social Reformer: Machiavelli and
Thomas More* (Houston: Rice Institute Pamphlet, 1957), pp. 7–8; Villari,
*Life,* I, 217–18; Whitfield, *Machiavelli,* pp. 83–91, and "Savonarola and
the Purpose of 'The Prince,' " *Modern Language Review* 44 (1949):44–59;
Donald Weinstein, "Machiavelli and Savonarola," in *Studies on Machiavelli,*
ed. Myron Gilmore (Florence, 1972), p. 25.

22. Gilbert, *The Chief Works,* III, 1448; *Il teatro e tutti gli scritti letterari,*
ed. F. Gaeta (Milan, 1965), p. 242.

23. Gilbert, *Letters,* pp. 147–48.

24. Ibid., p. 198.

25. *The Discourses of Niccolò Machiavelli,* trans. Leslie J. Walker I (New
Haven, 1950), pp. 242–43.

26. Ibid., pp. 313–14.

27. Ibid., p. 547; Tarlton, *Fortune's Circle,* pp. 57–59.

28. For opposing views see Whitfield, "Savonarola and the Purpose of
*The Prince,"* and Weinstein, "Machiavelli and Savonarola."

29. Weinstein, "Machiavelli and Savonarola," p. 261.

30. Ridolfi, *Life,* pp. 16, 262; Villari, *Life,* I, 221–22; Gaeta, *Lettere,*
pp. 28–29.

31. Nicolai Rubinstein, "The Beginnings of Niccolò Machiavelli's Career in the Florentine Chancery," *Italian Studies* 11 (1956):72–91, affirms

this date by his discovery of the register of *deliberazioni,* which recorded the chancery elections.

32. Hale, *Machiavelli,* pp. 7–10, 32–33; Villari, *Life,* I, 225–26; Ridolfi, *Life,* p. 20.

33. Fredi Chiappelli, "Machiavelli as Secretary," *Italian Quarterly* 53 (1970):27–44. In 1507 Machiavelli became secretary of the *Nove Della Milizia,* charged with implementing military reforms.

34. Ridolfi, *Life,* pp. 18–19; Villari, *Life,* I, 227–28.

35. Hale, *Machiavelli,* pp. 37–39; Whitfield, *Machiavelli,* pp. 39–40.

36. On the Pisan War and Paolo Vitelli see Guicciardini's *History;* Hale, *Machiavelli,* pp. 34–46.

37. Federico Chabod points to the eventual hallmarks of Machiavelli's style: linear thought approximated in a structure based on contrasting sentences; avoidance of "and" by substituting "or"; tone set by repetitive initial phrases; juxtaposition of contrasting words and images; polemical exchanges with a hypothetical interlocutor. *Scritti su Machiavelli* (Turin, 1964), pp. 200–201, 262–63.

38. F. Chiappelli, "Gli Scritti di Machiavelli Segretario," *Cultura e scuola* 33–34 (1970):242–49, demonstrates no difference between the "secretary" and the "writer" and deemphasizes limiting biographical data. Ben Lawton, "Note sugli 'Scritti di Governo' del Machiavelli," *Italianistica: Rivista di Letteratura Italiana* 1 (1972):506–19, analyzes structure in the first 153 letters included in Chiappelli's *Legazioni, Commissarie, Scritti di Governo,* 2 vols. (Bari, 1971 and 1973).

39. On the Borgias see E. R. Chamberlin, *The Fall of the House of Borgia* (New York: Dial Press, 1974).

40. Gennaro Sasso, *Machiavelli e Cesare Borgia* (Rome: Ateneo, 1966), pp. 3–30, explains Florence's fear of Cesare.

41. Chiappelli, *Legazioni,* II, 114–15; *Legazioni e commissarie,* I, ed. Sergio Bertelli (Milan, 1964), p. 257. On letters from this mission, see Sasso, *Machiavelli e Cesare Borgia,* pp. 31–48.

42. Chiappelli, *Legazioni,* II, 125; Bertelli, *Legazioni,* I, 267–68; Sasso, *Storia,* pp. 35–43.

43. Chiappelli, *Legazioni,* II, 247–48; Bertelli, *Legazioni,* I, 392–93.

44. Chiappelli, *Legazioni,* II, 363, 365; Bertelli, *Legazioni,* I, 501, 503.

45. Chiappelli, *Legazioni,* II, 370; Bertelli, *Legazioni,* I, 508–509.

46. The date of the *Description* is uncertain; Whitfield, *Machiavelli,* pp. 46–47; Gilbert, *The Chief Works,* I, 163.

47. Sydney Anglo, *Machiavelli: A Dissection* (New York, 1969), p. 42.

48. Sasso, *Machiavelli e Cesare Borgia*, pp. 59–60, 87; Peter E. Bondanella, *Machiavelli and the Art of Renaissance History* (Detroit, 1973), p. 44.

49. Details conflict with historical facts. Machiavelli's letter of January 20, 1503, summarizing events described in lost letters, shows how Borgia had conducted his operations so deceptively as to conceal his army's size.

50. Bondanella, *The Art of Renaissance History*, pp. 44–45.

51. Ibid., p. 44.

52. Gilbert, *The Chief Works*, I, 168. Compare this with Machiavelli's letter of January 20, 1503; the portrait here combined with that in the *Description* shows how he reworked history.

53. Alessandro Montevecchi, "Le prime operette di Machiavelli: elementi dello stile storico," *Convivium* 33 (1965):152–61.

54. Hayden White, *Metahistory: The Historical Imagination In Nineteenth Century Europe* (Baltimore: Johns Hopkins University Press, 1973), pp. 1–132, describes the levels of an historical account and constructs a typology of historiographical styles. The *Description* presents raw historical data, and the narrative, linguistic, and theoretical strategies for structuring it into a verbal model or icon.

55. Montevecchi, "Le prime operette," p. 157, for Plutarch's influence in including Vitellozzo's departing words.

56. Vallori's letter to Machiavelli on October 31, 1502. Gaeta, *Lettere*, pp. 92–93.

57. Bertelli, *Legazioni*, II, 580–600.

58. Rubenstein, "Machiavelli and the World of Florentine Politics," in *Studies on Machiavelli*, ed. M. Gilmore, p. 12, says the date was added later. Gilbert, *The Chief Works*, III, 1439, agrees.

59. Gilbert, *The Chief Works*, III, 1440.

60. Ibid., p. 1443.

61. Ibid., I, 447; *Discourses*, I, 38, 5–7; II, 23, 1–6; III, 6, 43–45.

62. *Arte della guerra e scritti politici minori*, ed. Sergio Bertelli (Milan, 1961), p. 67. Gilbert, *The Chief Works*, I, 161, dates it in the 1520s.

*Chapter Two*

1. Gilbert, *Letters*, pp. 140–43; Gaeta, *Lettere*, pp. 301–306.

2. *Discourses* I, 17–18; Sasso, *Storia*, pp. 187–303.

3. F. Chabod, "Sulla composizione de *Il principe*," *Archivium Romanicum* 11 (1927):330–83; Hans Baron, "The *Principe* and the Puzzle of the Date of the *Discorsi*," *Bibliothèque d'Humanisme et Renaissance* 18 (1956):405–28; Felix Gilbert, "The Composition and Structure of Machiavelli's *Discorsi*,"

*Journal of the History of Ideas* 14 (1953):135–56; J. H. Hexter, "Seyssel, Machiavelli and Polybius VI: The Mystery of the Missing Translation," *Studies in the Renaissance* 3 (1956):75–96; C. H. Clough, "Yet Again Machiavelli's Prince," *Annali-Istituto Universitario Orientale di Napoli, sez. rom.* (1963):201–26.

4. The dedication imitates Isocrates' *Address to Nicocles,* one of the earliest examples of princely literature. In "Yet Again Machiavelli's Prince," p. 221, Clough says Machiavelli delayed in presenting *The Prince* to Giuliano because he feared his contemporaries would think he was writing to teach princes methods of tyranny, rather than to outline a concept of an Italian confederation of states within which Florence would retain her republican government. Prezzolini, *Machiavelli,* p. 163, recalls Machiavelli's answer to a man who had accused him of teaching tyrants the art of conquering power: "True . . . but I have taught nations as well the art of conquering tyrants."

5. Allan H. Gilbert, *Machiavelli's Prince and Its Forerunners* (Durham, N.C., 1938).

6. Francis Bacon, *The Advancement of Learning,* ed. G. W. Kitchin (rpt. New York: E. P. Dutton, 1958), p. 24.

7. D. Carozza, "Il capitolo ventiseisimo del *Principe: Sintesi del l'opera,*" *Forum Italicum* 1 (1965):195–96; Russo, *Machiavelli,* pp. 68–72; L. Olschki, *Machiavelli, the Scientist* (Berkeley: Gillick Press, 1945), pp. 10–11; E. Girardi, "Unità, genesi e struttura del *Principe,*" *Lettere italiane* 22 (1970):3–30.

8. John H. Geerken, "Homer's Image of the Hero in Machiavelli: A Comparison of *Arete* and *Virtù,*" *Italian Quarterly* 53 (1970):45–90.

9. Ernst Robert Curtius, *European Literature and the Latin Middle Ages,* trans. Willard R. Trask (rpt. New York: Harper and Row, 1963), pp. 167–82.

10. Bertrand Russell, *A History of Western Philosophy* (New York: Simon and Schuster, 1945), pp. 761–62.

11. David E. Ingersoll, "The Constant Prince: Private Interests and Public Goals in Machiavelli," *Western Political Quarterly* 21 (1968):588–96, discusses the prince's glory.

12. Clough, "Political Assumptions and Objectives," p. 49.

13. Gilbert, *The Chief Works,* I, 58; F. Gilbert, "Humanist Conception of the Prince and *The Prince* of Machiavelli," *Journal of Modern History* 11 (1939):449–83.

14. J. A. Mazzeo, "Machiavelli: The Artist as Statesman," *University of Toronto Quarterly* 31 (April 1962):265–82; Neal Wood, "Machiavelli's Concept of *Virtù* Reconsidered," *Political Studies* 15 (1967):159–72; Fried-

rich Meinecke, *Machiavellism: The Doctrine of Raison d'État and Its Place in Modern History*, trans. Douglas Scott (London, 1957); Karl von Vorys, "The Political Sociology of Machiavelli," *Bucknell Review* 9 (1961):318–32; F. Gilbert, "On Machiavelli's Idea of *Virtù*," *Renaissance News* 4 (Winter 1951):53–55; Gioacchino Paparelli, "Virtù e fortuna nel medioevo, nel Rinascimento e nel Machiavelli," *Cultura e scuola* 33–34 (1970):76–89; Felice Alderisio, *Machiavelli: L'arte dello stato nell' azione e negli scritti* (Turin: Fratelli, 1930). Machiavelli's fullest discussion of *virtù* is in *The Art of War*.

15. Wood, "Machiavelli's Concept of *'Virtù'* Reconsidered," pp. 161–62, reaches interesting conclusions about Machiavelli's heroes.

16. Gilbert, *The Chief Works*, I, 28–29.

17. Clough, "Yet Again Machiavelli's Prince," pp. 213–15.

18. Gilbert, *The Chief Works*, I, 31.

19. Northrop Frye, "New Directions From Old," *Myth and Myth-making*, ed. Henry A. Murray (New York: George Braziller, 1960), pp. 117–18, defines metahistory, history, and poetry.

20. Machiavelli's method resembles that of the "right poets," described by Sidney in *An Apology for Poetry* (1591), who feign images of virtues and vices for the purpose of teaching delightfully. *Sir Philip Sidney's Defense of Poesy*, ed. Lewis Soens (Lincoln: University of Nebraska Press, 1970), p. 13.

21. Mary Barnard, *The Mythmakers* (Athens: Ohio University Press, 1966), pp. 39–49, explains the shaman as actor.

22. John T. Marcus, "The World Impact of the West: The Mystique and the Sense of Participation in History," in *Myth and Myth-making*, ed. Henry A. Murray, pp. 221–39, defines "mystique-sense" as ". . . the identification of an historical ideal with an historical event, and conversely, the transmutation of an historical event into an historical ideal." Such is the effect of Machiavelli's portrayal of his four paragons and new prince.

23. Barnard, *The Mythmakers*, p. 4.

24. Von Vorys, "The Political Sociology of Machiavelli."

25. Prezzolini, *Machiavelli*, p. 20.

26. Joseph Campbell, "Mythological Themes in Creative Literature and Art," in his edition of *Myths, Dreams, and Religion* (New York: Dutton, 1970), p. 145.

27. Gilbert, *The Chief Works*, I, 58–59. On ethics see Isaiah Berlin, "The Originality of Machiavelli," in *Studies on Machiavelli*, ed. M. Gilmore, pp. 147–206; Delio Cantimori, "Machiavelli e la religione," *Belfagor* 21 (1966):629–38; Alberto Tenenti, "La religione di Machiavelli," *Studi storici* 10 (1969):709–48.

28. Gilbert, *The Chief Works*, I, 66–67.

29. W. R. Campbell, *Machiavelli: An Anti-Study* (Kingston: University of Rhode Island Press, 1968), pp. 46–47, says Agathocles committed evil out of prudence, while Moses, etc., did so out of benevolence.

30. We must distinguish between his personal and political views of religion.

31. Felix Gilbert, "Florentine Political Assumptions in the Period of Savonarola and Soderini," *Journal of the Warburg and Courtauld Institutes* 20 (1957):187–214.

32. Gilbert, *The Chief Works*, I, 20.

33. Ibid., p. 44.

34. Von Vorys, "The Political Sociology of Man," p. 327.

35. Gilbert, *The Chief Works*, I, 27.

36. Garrett Mattingly, "Machiavelli's *Prince:* Political Science or Political Satire?" *American Scholar* 27 (1958):482–91, sees the work as satire. Clough, "Yet Again Machiavelli's Prince," pp. 210–11, disagrees. The improbability of it as satire does not obviate the structural and thematic use of satire and irony.

37. Gilbert, *The Chief Works*, I, 25; Bruno Di Porto, "Il problema religioso in Machiavelli," *Idea* 21 (1965):245–50.

38. See Moses in Sigmund Freud, *Moses and Monotheism*, trans. Katherine Jones (New York: Vintage Books, 1939).

39. Francesco DeSanctis, *The History of Italian Literature*, 2 vols., trans. Joan Redfern (New York, 1959), pp. 537–58.

40. Soens, *Sir Philip Sidney's Defense of Poesy*, pp. 11–13. Charles D. Tarlton, "The Symbolism of Redemption and the Exorcism of Fortune in Machiavelli's Prince," *Review of Politics* 30 (July 1968):332–48, analyzes it as a symbolic poetic structure.

41. De Sanctis, *History of Italian Literature*, p. 558.

42. J. H. Whitfield, "On Machiavelli's Use of 'Ordini,' " *Italian Studies* 10 (1955):19–39; Renzo Zanon, "Parole del Machiavelli: Populo," *Lingua Nostra* 30 (1969):101–105; Fredi Chiappelli, *Studi sul linguaggio del Machiavelli* (Florence, 1952); Cecil Grayson, "Lorenzo, Machiavelli and the Italian Language," in *Italian Renaissance Studies*, ed. E. F. Jacob, pp. 410–32.

43. J. H. Hexter, "The Loom of Language and the Fabric of Imperatives: The Case of *Il Principe* and *Utopia*," *American Historical Review* 69 (1964):965–68.

44. Domenico Cernecca, "Il costrutto predicativo nella prosa del *Principe*," *Studi di grammatica Italiana* 1 (1971):101–16; Mario Olivieri, "La

tecnica politica nel *Principe* di Niccolò Machiavelli," *Filosofia* 20 (1969):563–64.

45. Delio Cantimori, "Rhetoric and Politics in Italian Humanism," *Journal of the Warburg and Courtauld Institutes* 1 (1937–38):83–102, for the relationship of Florentine humanists such as Orti Oricellari group to the humanist tradition.

46. Hanna H. Gray, "Renaissance Humanism: The Pursuit of Eloquence," *Journal of the History of Ideas* 24 (1963):497–514.

47. The didacticism of eloquence relates to Machiavelli's view of corruption. See Alfredo Bonadeo, *Corruption, Conflict and Power in the Works and Times of Niccolò Machiavelli* (Berkeley: University of California Press, 1973).

48. Gray, "Renaissance Humanism," pp. 505–506, shows the influence of Cicero's *De Oratore*.

49. Olschki, *Machiavelli, the Scientist;* Aldo Scaglione, "Machiavelli the Scientist?" *Symposium* 10 (1956):243–50.

50. Thomas Wheeler, "The Fascination of *Il Principe*," *Renaissance Papers 1975*, ed. D. G. Donovan and A. Leigh Deneef (Durham, N.C.: The Southeastern Renaissance Conference, 1976), pp. 29–35.

51. Tarlton, "The Symbolism of Redemption."

*Chapter Three*

1. Hans Baron, "Machiavelli: the Republican Citizen and the Author of *The Prince*," *English Historical Review* 76 (1961):217–53, summarizes the history of this question in Europe.

2. Ridolfi, *Life*, pp. 148–54, 301.

3. Gilbert, *The Chief Works*, I, 11. See note 3, ch. 2.

4. Baron, "The *Principe* and the Puzzle of the Date of the *Discorsi*," and "Machiavelli: the Republican Citizen and the Author of *The Prince*"; F. Gilbert, "The Composition and Structure of Machiavelli's *Discorsi*," charts the references to Livy, concluding there were two stages in its composition; Sasso, "Intorno alla Composizione dei 'Discorsi' di Niccolò Machiavelli," *Giornale storico della letteratura italiana* 134 (1957):482–534, and 135 (1958):215–59; Whitfield, "Discourses on Machiavelli VII: Gilbert, Hexter, and Baron," *Italian Studies* 13 (1958):21–46.

5. Walker, *Discourses*, I, 202. References to the *Discourses* are taken from this translation, although I have also consulted Gilbert, *The Chief Works*, I, and the Italian edition, Bertelli, *Il Principe e Discorsi*.

6. Pulver, *Machiavelli*, p. 233.

7. Clough, "Yet Again Machiavelli's *Prince,*" pp. 212–13; Sasso, *Studi su Machiavelli* (Naples: Morano, 1967), p. 107.

8. Baron, "Machiavelli: the Republican Citizen and the Author of *The Prince,*" p. 228.

9. F. Gilbert, "The Composition and Structure of Machiavelli's *Discorsi,*" pp. 143–50.

10. Russo, *Machiavelli,* pp. 53–58.

11. On "liberty" see Marcia L. Colish, "The Idea of Liberty in Machiavelli," *Journal of the History of Ideas* 32 (1971):323–50; Giorgio Cadoni, "Libertà, repubblica e governo misto in Machiavelli," *Revista internazionale della filosofia del diritto* 39 (1962):462–84, and "Genesi e crisi del 'vivere libero' in Machiavelli," *Rivista internazionale di filosofia del diritto* 42 (1965):106–45.

12. Tarlton, *Fortune's Circle,* pp. 146–49; Mario Martelli, "Popolo e principe in Niccolò Machiavelli," *Belfagor* 14 (1959):447–53, on the heroes in both works.

13. Guicciardini used the autograph manuscript for his *Considerations on the 'Discourses' of Machiavelli.* Peter E. Bondanella, *Francesco Guicciardini* (Boston: Twayne, 1976), p. 61.

14. Walker, *Discourses,* I, 57–59; J. G. A. Pocock, *The Machiavellian Moment: Florentine Political Thought and the Atlantic Republican Tradition* (Princeton, N.J., 1975), pp. 199–203.

15. Walker, *Discourses,* I, 205–206.

16. Ibid., pp. 353–56.

17. Carlo Pincin, "Le prefazioni e la dedicatoria dei *Discorsi* di Machiavelli," *Giornale storico della letteratura italiana* 143 (1966):72–83, analyzes manuscript changes.

18. On Machiavelli's sources see Walker, *Discourses,* I, 89–93; II, 271–305; Harvey C. Mansfield, "Machiavelli's New Regime," *Italian Quarterly* 52 (1970):63–96; Leo Strauss, *Thoughts on Machiavelli* (Seattle, 1958), pp. 85–173; Brian Richardson, "Notes on Machiavelli's Sources," *Italian Studies* 26 (1971):24–48.

19. Strauss, *Thoughts,* pp. 440–41; Walker, *Discourses,* I, 80–93.

20. B. Richardson, "The Structure of Machiavelli's *Discorsi,*" *Italica* 49 (1972):460–71, studies Machiavelli's originality.

21. Walker, *Discourses,* I, 165–98, provides a useful analytical table of contents for each book.

22. John Plamenatz, "In Search of Machiavellian *Virtù,*" in *The Political Calculus,* ed. Anthony Parel (Toronto, 1972), pp. 157–78; Walker, *Discourses,* I, 99–102.

23. Walker, *Discourses,* I, 498; Thomas Flanagan, "The Concept of *Fortuna* in Machiavelli," in *The Political Calculus,* ed. Anthony Parel, pp. 127–56.

24. G. S. Rousseau, "The *Discorsi* of Machiavelli: History and Theory," *Cahiers d'histoire mondiale* 9 (1965):143–61; Dante Germino, "Machiavelli's Thoughts on the Psyche and Society," in *The Political Calculus,* ed. Anthony Parel, pp. 59–82; Walker, *Discourses,* I, 128–34, 135–36.

25. Alfredo Bonadeo, "The Role of the People in the Works and Times of Machiavelli," *Bibliothèque d'Humanisme et Renaissance* 32 (1970):351–77; Walker, *Discourses,* I, 147.

26. Germino, "Machiavelli's Thoughts on the Psyche and Society"; Rousseau, "The *Discorsi* of Machiavelli"; Gennaro Sasso, "Polibio e Machiavelli," *Giornale critico della filosofia italiana* 15 (1961):51–86.

27. Walker, *Discourses,* I, 114–18; Leo Strauss, "Walker's Machiavelli," *Review of Metaphysics* 6 (1953):437–46; Harvey Mansfield, Jr., "Necessity in the Beginnings of Cities," in *The Political Calculus,* ed. Anthony Parel, pp. 101–25; Rousseau, "The *Discorsi* of Machiavelli," pp. 150–52.

28. Strauss, *Thoughts,* pp. 85–173.

29. Harvey Mansfield, Jr., "Necessity in the Beginnings of Cities," in *The Political Calculus,* ed. Anthony Parel, pp. 104–107, says Machiavelli's use of rhetoric makes him more a poet than a philosopher. See F. Gilbert, *Machiavelli and Guicciardini: Politics and History in Sixteenth Century Florence* (Princeton, N.J., 1965), p. 193, and Ridolfi, *Life,* pp. 13, 107, 168, 252.

30. Bondanella, *Machiavelli and the Art of Renaissance History,* pp. 60–68.

31. Strauss, *Thoughts,* pp. 139–48.

32. Rousseau, "The *Discorsi* of Machiavelli," p. 145.

*Chapter Four*

1. Sasso, *Storia,* pp. 422–35.

2. Charles C. Bayley, *War and Society in Renaissance Florence: "De Militia" of Leonardo Bruni* (Toronto: University of Toronto Press, 1961), pp. 240–315; *The Art of War,* intro. by Neal Wood (Indianapolis, 1965), pp. xi–xvi; J. R. Hale, "War and Public Opinion in Renaissance Italy," in *Italian Renaissance Studies,* ed. E. F. Jacob, pp. 94–122.

3. Arthur Burd, "Le fonti letterarie di Machiavelli nell' *Arte della Guerra,*" *Atti della Reale Accademia dei Lincei,* Series 5, vol. 4 (1896): pt. 1, 187–261; Wood, *The Art of War,* pp. xvi–xxv; Wood's "Frontinus as a Possible Source for Machiavelli's Method," *Journal of the History of Ideas*

28 (1967):243–48, discusses Julius Sextus Frontinus' *Stratagemata* (A.D. 1) as a source.

4. Felix Gilbert, *Niccolò Machiavelli e la vita culturale del suo tempo* (Bologna, 1969), p. 222.

5. Joseph Kraft, "Truth and Poetry in Machiavelli," *Journal of Modern History* 23 (1951):109–21, discusses the scientific and poetical in *The Art of War* but lacks sensitivity to rhetorical intentions and methods. He disassociates Machiavelli from political implications, seeing him as military strategist rather than as imaginative artist. My discussion intends to summarize important technical aspects, and more essentially to illuminate neglected rhetorical and literary aspects.

6. See Hoffman Nickerson, "Warfare in the Roman Empire, the Dark and Middle Ages, to 1494 A.D.," in *Warfare: A Study of Military Methods from the Earliest Times,* ed. O. L. Spaulding, H. Nickerson, J. W. Wright (New York: Harcourt, Brace and Co., 1925), pp. 191–496.

7. *Arte della guerra e scritti politici minori,* ed. Sergio Bertelli, pp. 309–12.

8. Gray, "Renaissance Humanism"; Cantimori, "Rhetoric and Politics," connects Antonio Brucioli's *Dialoghi della morale filosofia* (Venice, 1526), Florentine rhetorical humanism, the Orti group, and Renaissance political writing as a whole.

9. Cantimori, "Rhetoric and Politics," p. 98, points out an opposing view on the defects of oratory. Machiavelli reveals aspects from this view, particularly his use of the "vulgar tongue" to speak of politics.

10. My analysis compares the Bertelli Italian edition with the Farneworth translation (Wood, *The Art of War*) and with Gilbert's translation in *The Chief Works,* II.

11. Gilbert, *The Chief Works,* II, 570.

12. Gray, "Renaissance Humanism," p. 505.

13. Gilbert, *The Chief Works,* II, 570–71.

14. Ibid., p. 572.

15. Wood, *The Art of War,* "Introduction," p. xxxi.

16. Villari, *Life,* II, 308–11. One thousand were armed with the *scoppietto* or matchlock, a new small arm, and positioned with the artillery; 70 percent of the remaining infantry had pikes and 20 percent spears, halberds, swords, or crossbows. See Allan H. Gilbert, "Machiavelli on Fire Weapons," *Italica* 23 (1946):275–86.

17. F. Gilbert, *Niccolò Machiavelli e la vita culturale,* pp. 214–18.

18. Gilbert, *The Chief Works,* II, 634–35.

19. A. Gilbert, "Machiavelli on Fire Weapons," corrects misconceptions about Machiavelli's disparagement of new weapons. See Rodolfo De Mattei, "Machiavelli e L'Europa," *Cultura e scuola* 5 (1966):82–91.

20. Olschki, *Machiavelli, the Scientist,* pp. 50–51; F. Gilbert, *Niccolò Machiavelli e la vita culturale,* pp. 210–12, explains Machiavelli's attitude on money in war; it could assist but not assure conquest, especially with the moral and political corruption which materialism and progress fostered.

21. Villari, *Life,* II, 313–15.

22. Gilbert, *The Chief Works,* II, 724.

23. Ibid., p. 726.

24. Wood, *The Art of War,* "Introduction," pp. xxix–xxx, ixxxiv–ixxxvi.

25. Wood begins this in his "Introduction," pp. xxv–xivii.

*Chapter Five*

1. Hale, *Machiavelli,* pp. 47–54; Whitfield, *Machiavelli,* pp. 40–44; Sasso, *Storia,* pp. 27–35.

2. Sasso, *Storia,* p. 34.

3. F. Gilbert, "Machiavelli's *Istorie fiorentine,"* in *Studies on Machiavelli,* ed. M. Gilmore, p. 75.

4. Guido Guarino, "Two Views of a Renaissance Tyrant," *Symposium* 10 (1956):285–86; Vittorio Turri, *Machiavelli* (Florence: G. Barbera, 1902), p. 166; Eric Voegelin, "Machiavelli's *Prince:* Background and Formation," *Review of Politics* 5 (1951):165.

5. F. Gilbert, *Machiavelli and Guicciardini;* Gray, "Renaissance Humanism"; Voegelin, "Machiavelli's *Prince";* Bondanella, *Machiavelli and the Art of Renaissance History;* Donald J. Wilcox, *The Development of Florentine Humanist Historiography in the Fifteenth Century* (Cambridge: Harvard University Press, 1969).

6. Voegelin, "Machiavelli's *Prince,"* p. 152; *The History of Florence and Other Selections,* ed. M. P. Gilmore, trans. Judith A. Rawson (New York, 1970), pp. xxix–xxxiii.

7. *History of Florence and of the Affairs of Italy,* ed. Felix Gilbert (New York: Harper and Row, 1960), pp. xii–xiii.

8. See Eduardo Fueter, *Storia della storiografia moderna,* trans. A. Spinelli (Naples: Ricciardi, 1943), I, 67–73; Franco Gaeta, "Machiavelli lo storico," *Terzo programma* 10 (1970):40–48, compares the historian, legislator, orator, and poet.

9. F. Gilbert, "Machiavelli's *Istorie fiorentine,* pp. 92–99; Walker, *Discourses* I, ii; Gilbert, *The Chief Works,* III, 1027–35.

10. F. Gilbert, pp. 94–95.

11. Clough, "Political Assumptions and Objectives."

12. Gaeta, *Lettere*, pp. 394–95; F. Gilbert, "Machiavelli's *Istorie fiorentine*," p. 79. Machiavelli's letter of August 29, 1520 which accompanied *The Life* has been lost.

13. Gilbert, *The Chief Works*, II, 534.

14. Machiavelli's account is based on several sources, the most modern being Niccolò Tegrimi, *Vita Castruccii Antelminelli Lucensis Ducis* (1494). Guarino, "Two Views of a Renaissance Tyrant," compares Tegrimi's history with Machiavelli's artistic version. See G. Simonetti, "I biografi de Castruccio Castracani," *Studi storici* 2 (1893):1–24.

15. Hale, *Machiavelli*, pp. 200–201, says the commission avoids the all-inclusive term *istorie*, which comprised interpretation and facts. F. Gilbert, "Machiavelli's *Istorie fiorentine*," shows how the commission shaped its content. Florence followed Venice's precedent of appointing Andrea Navagero as historian in 1516 at a salary. The Medici appointment of Machiavelli for a fee was a novelty in Florence, since all previous historiographers (Bruni and Poggio) wrote voluntarily and without pay.

16. Ridolfi, *Life*, pp. 197–98, on their availability to Machiavelli.

17. F. Gilbert, "Machiavelli's *Istorie fiorentine*," pp. 87–92, discusses Book I within the whole structure, showing it may belong to a later stage in composition.

18. Ibid., pp. 81–85, analyzes the compositional method.

19. Ibid., pp. 85–87, shows how Machiavelli's feelings surface in the speeches, how he intended to portray the abasement of Florentine civic life under Medici rule, how wealth, the merchant class, and arts and letters eventually brought the collapse of "heroic virtues."

20. Gilbert, *Letters*, p. 206.

21. Fueter, *Storia della storiografia moderna*, I, 82–83.

22. F. Gilbert, *Machiavelli and Guicciardini*, pp. 160–72. See *Discourses* I, 37, 49, 52; III, 3, 28, 46, on the aristocracy.

*Chapter Six*

1. English citations from the plays refer to Gilbert, *The Chief Works*, II. Comparisons are made with the Italian, Gaeta, *Il teatro*, and with other English translations such as *Mandragola*, trans. Anne Paolucci and Henry Paolucci (Indianapolis, 1957) and *Mandragola*, trans. Mera J. Flaumenaft (Prospect Heights, Il., 1980).

2. Ridolfi, *Life*, pp. 301–306.

3. R. Ridolfi, "Composizione, rappresentazione, prima edizione della *Mandragola*," *La Bibliofilia* 64 (1962):285–300.

4. Sergio Bertelli, "When Did Machiavelli Write *Mandragola?*" Renaissance Quarterly 24 (1971):317–26, bases this view on Kenneth M. Setton, "Pope Leo X and the Turkish Peril," Penrose Memorial Lecture, *Proceedings of the American Philosophical Society* 113 (1969):377. See Allan Gilbert, "The Dates of *Clizia* and *Mandragola,*" *PMLA* 64 (1949):1231–35.

5. Antonio Parronchi, "La prima rappresentazione della *Mandragola*. Il modello dell' apparato. L'allegoria," *La Bibliofilia* 64 (1962):37–86, claims discovery of the sceneries used for the plays, including that for the September 7, 1518, performance of *Mandragola*. The plays performed on the subsequent days were the lost *Falargo* and *La Pisana* attributed to Leonardo Strozzi.

6. R. Ridolfi, *La Mandragola. Per la prima volta restituita alla sua integrità* (Florence: Olschki, 1965); "Tradizione manoscritta della *Mandragola,*" *La Bibliofilia* 67 (1965):1–16; "Composizione, rappresentazione, prima edizione della *Mandragola.*" His findings have been qualified by Fredi Chiappelli, "Considerazioni di linguaggio e stile della *Mandragola,*" *Giornale storico della letteratura italiana* 146 (1969):252–59, and "Sulla composizione della *Mandragola,*" *Approdo* 32 (1965):79–84; and by Vincenzo Romano, "Niccolò Machiavelli. *La mandragola* per la prima volta restituita alla sua integrità. A cura di Roberto Ridolfi," *Belfagor* 21 (1966):614–21; see Fifi-Dolores Colimore, "Edizioni e traduzioni della *Mandragola,*" *Italica* 18 (1941):55–59.

7. Bertelli, "When Did Machiavelli Write *Mandragola?*", pp. 317–18. Giorgio Padoan, *"La mandragola* del Machiavelli nella Venezia cinquecentesca," *Lettere italiane* 22 (1970):161–86, analyzes how Sanudo's entry reflects Venetian response to the play.

8. The speaker's quip that future settings will be Rome and Pisa coincides with the settings of the next two plays performed on the successive days of Lorenzo's marriage festivities.

9. Apparently in 1504 Machiavelli wrote a play entitled *Le maschere* which his grandson, Giuliano de' Ricci, destroyed for its invective against contemporary Florentines.

10. Machiavelli's prose translation of Terence's *Andria* (date uncertain, but probably between 1515 and 1518, before the *Mandragola*) may have resulted from this interest. It represents an early step toward the comic theory based on language. Publio Filippo Mantovano's *Formicone* (performed in Mantua in 1503) may be the first learned comedy. See Marvin T. Herrick, *Italian Comedy in the Renaissance* (Urbana: University of Illinois Press, 1966), pp. 60–164.

11. Edwin J. Webber, "The Dramatic Unities in the 'Mandragola,' " *Italica* 33 (1956):20–21, shows how Machiavelli anticipated the views of Robertelli, Segni, Trissino, and Castelvetro.

12. Luigi Russo, *Commedie Fiorentine del '500* (Florence: Sansoni, 1939), pp. 26–38; Franco Fido, "Machiavelli 1469–1969: Politica e teatro nel badalucco di Messer Nicia," *Italica* 46 (1969):363–64.

13. Theodore A. Sumberg, *"La mandragola:* An Interpretation," *Journal of Politics* 2 (1961):320–40, interprets it as political allegory. Parronchi, "La prima rappresentazione," pp. 59–69, endorses it as an allegory of the Medici return to Florence: Callimaco represents Lorenzo; Nicia, Soderini; Lucrezia, Florence, etc.

14. Fido, "Machiavelli 1469–1969," pp. 359–75, traces the play's critical reception.

15. Robert I. Williams, "Machiavelli's *Mandragola,* Touchwood Senior, and the Comedy of Middleton's *A Chaste Maid in Cheapside,*" *Studies in English Literature* 10 (1970):385–96, does not recognize that just as Middleton's play is a humorous portrayal of English middle-class society, the *Mandragola* likewise is a satire on Florentine middle-class mores.

16. Gaeta, *Il teatro,* pp. 196–97.

17. Charles S. Singleton, "Machiavelli and the Spirit of Comedy," *Modern Language Notes* 57 (1942):585–92, demonstrates how the old woman in III.3 of the *Mandragola* symbolizes its "local texture" and comic vision. Nino Borsellino, "Per una storia delle commedie di Machiavelli," *Cultura e scuola* 33–34 (1970):229–41, has more on language.

18. See Martin Fleisher, "Trust and Deceit in Machiavelli's Comedies," *Journal of the History of Ideas* 27 (1966):365–80.

19. Beatrice Corrigan, "An Unrecorded Manuscript of Machiavelli's *La Clizia,*" *La Bibliofilia* 62 (1961):73–87; Frank Allan Thomson, "The Significance of the Colchester Clizia MS.," *Fairbanks Essays* 27 (1966):121–35; Roberto Ridolfi, "La *Clizia* di Machiavelli," *Veltro* 4 (1960):5–8, and "Contributo a un'edizione critica della *Clizia,*" *La Bibliofilia* 69 (1967):91–101.

20. *Clizia,* trans. Oliver Evans, "Introduction" (Great Neck, N.Y., 1962), pp. 2–15.

21. Allan H. Gilbert, "The Dates of *Clizia* and *Mandragola,*" p. 1232, outlines plot relationships.

22. Gilbert, *The Chief Works,* II, 861; Gaeta, *Il teatro,* p. 162.

23. Allan Gilbert, "Machiavelli as Poet," *South Atlantic Studies for Sturgis E. Leavitt* (Washington, D.C.: South Atlantic Modern Language Association, 1953), pp. 163–74, uses the poetry as a springboard for discussion of *The Prince.*

24. Anthony Parel, "Machiavelli Minore," in *The Political Calculus,* pp. 183–84, discusses the influence of these writers.

25. Joseph Tusiani, "The Poetry of Machiavelli," *Literary Review* 6 (1963):392–96.

26. The no longer extant Vespucci edition was described by Giuseppe Torre, *Il Bibliofilo* 2 (1881):76–77. An early pirated edition was done by Andrea Ghirlandi da Pistoia and Antonio Tubini. For the early editions of the first *Decennale,* see E. H. Wilkins, W. A. Jackson, and R. H. Rouse, *Niccolò Machiavelli: The First Decennale, A facsimile of the first edition of February, 1506* (Cambridge: Harvard University Press, 1969). Allusions to the *Decennali* refer to Gilbert, *The Chief Works,* III, 1444–61; Gaeta, *Il teatro,* pp. 233–66; and *Lust and Liberty: The Poems of Machiavelli,* trans. Joseph Tusiani (New York, 1963), pp. 152–80.

27. Gilbert, *The Chief Works,* III, 1453.

28. Gilbert, *The Chief Works,* II, 744. See *Discourses* I, 28–32, for more on Machiavelli's views on Ingratitude.

29. Gilbert, *The Chief Works,* II, 735; Tusiani, *Lust and Liberty,* p. 192.

30. Tusiani, *Lust and Liberty,* pp. 128, 193–94; Gaeta, *Il teatro,* p. 325.

31. Gilbert, *The Chief Works,* II, 750–72; Tusiani, *Lust and Liberty,* pp. 51–100, 187–90; Gaeta, *Il teatro,* pp. 269–302.

32. Tusiani, *Lust and Liberty,* p. 190; Elizabeth Barker, "Gelli's *Circe* and Jonathan Swift," *Cesare Barbieri Courier* 2 (November 1959):3–15; Emmanuel Hatzantonis, "Il potere metamorfico di Circe quale motivo satirico in Machiavelli, Gelli, e Bruno," *Italica* 37 (1960):257–68; Fernando Figurelli, "Ancora sul verseggiatore," *Cultura e scuola* 33–34 (1970):192–215.

*Chapter Seven*

1. The most comprehensive treatment is Franco Fido, *Machiavelli: Storia della critica* (Palermo, 1965).

2. Ernst Cassirer, *The Myth of the State* (New Haven: Yale University Press, 1946), p. 120, says, ". . . Machiavelli was no Machiavellian," his life did not conform to the distorted view, and he was ". . . perhaps one of the most sincere political writers."

3. Antonio Panella, *Gli antimachiavellici* (Florence: Sansoni, 1943), p. 16, points out that Machiavelli may have been the purist of the so-called Anti-Machiavellians.

4. Ridolfi, *Life,* pp. 12, 260–61, for how Machiavellism was influenced by iconography, as indicated also by Tommasini, *La vita,* I, 64–70;

II, 958. See T. B. Macauley's physical description of Machiavelli in "Milton
and Machiavelli," in his *Historical Essays* (New York, 1921), p. 401.
    5. Clough, "Political Assumptions and Objectives," p. 30.
    6. Luigi Firpo, "Le origini dell'antimachiavellismo," *Pensiero politico*
2 (1969):355–56; G. B. Busini, *Lettere a Benedetto Varchi sopra l'assedio di
Firenze,* ed. G. Milanesi (Florence: Le Monnier, 1860), pp. 84–85.
    7. Mario D'Addio, "Machiavelli e Antimachiavelli," *Pensiero politico*
2 (1969):329–36, for how the Counterreformation tried to restore rapport
between ethics and politics which *The Prince* seemed to dissolve.
    8. Antonio Possevino (1534–1611), a Jesuit, included Machiavelli and
Gentillet in his *Iudicium de Nicolao Machiavello* (1592) as two heretical
writers he condemned. See Fido, *Machiavelli,* pp. 13–15, for other Renaissance Catholic theologians who opposed Machiavelli.
    9. Salvo Mastellone, "Antimachiavellismo, machiavellismo, e taci-
tismo," *Cultura e scuola* 33–34 (1970):132–38, outlines the Huguenot
origins of Anti-Machiavellism.
    10. Clough, "Political Assumptions and Objectives," pp. 52–54,
points out that Nifo's plagiarism shows how *The Prince* was untypical of
treatises on princely duty.
    11. Prezzolini, *Machiavelli,* p. 213; Firpo, "Le origini dell' antima-
chiavellismo"; Andrea Sorrentino, *Storia sull'antimachiavellismo Europeo*
(Naples: Loffredo, 1936), pp. 6–30.
    12. Fido, *Machiavelli,* p. 8.
    13. Randolph Starn, "Ante Machiavel: Machiavelli and Giannotti," in
*Studies on Machiavelli,* ed. Myron Gilmore, pp. 285–93.
    14. Bondanella, *Guicciardini,* pp. 61–74; Rodolfo De Mattei, "Distin-
zioni in sede di antimachiavellismo," *Pensiero politico* 2 (1970):368–75;
Clough, "Political Assumptions and Objectives," pp. 63–65; Firpo, "Le
origini dell'antimachiavellismo," pp. 358–63; Ridolfi, *Life,* pp. 186–215;
Roberto Ridolfi, *The Life of Francesco Guicciardini,* trans. Cecil Grayson
(New York: Knopf, 1968).
    15. Prezzolini, *Machiavelli,* pp. 25–40.
    16. Ibid., pp. 218–25; Fido, *Machiavelli,* pp. 20–35; Rodolfo De
Mattei, "La sopravvivenza del Machiavelli nel pensiero politico del sei-
cento," *Storia e politica* 7 (1968):343–56; F. Gaeta, *Il pensiero politico di
Machiavelli e la sua fortuna nel mondo* (Florence: Instituto Nazionale di Studi
sul Rinascimento, 1972); Michele Ciliberto, "Appunti per una storia della
fortuna di Machiavelli in Italia: F. Ercole e L. Russo," *Studi storici* 10
(1969):799–832. See Karl Ludwig Selig, "An Anti-Machiavellian Emblem," *Italica* 38 (1961):134–35, for an emblem with its accompanying

162 NICCOLÒ MACHIAVELLI

Latin poem as it appeared in Henricus Oraeus, *Viridarium hieroglyphico morale* (Frankfurt, 1619), p. 90.

17. Émile Namer, "Machiavel et Giambattista Vico," *Notiziario culturale italiano* 10 (March-April 1966):1–10; Benedetto Croce, *Machiavelli e Vico. La politica e l'etica* (Bari: Laterza, 1925).

18. Fido, *Machiavelli*, pp. 49–76. The oblique interpretation of *The Prince* ironically furthered the "Machiavellian legend."

19. Ibid., pp. 78–85; De Sanctis, *The History of Italian Literature;* Giuliano Procacci, *Studi sulla fortuna del Machiavelli* (Rome: Tipografia S. Pio, 1965), pp. 442–50.

20. Fido, *Machiavelli*, pp. 86–94.

21. Ibid., pp. 95–98.

22. Ibid., pp. 100–106.

23. Procacci, *Studi sulla fortuna del Machiavelli*, pp. 442–50. Gentillet's claim that Machiavelli had been imported into France by the Florentines was incorrect. On early French anti-Machiavellism, see Pamela D. Stewart, *Innocent Gentillet e la sua polemica antimachiavellica* (Florence: Nuova Italia, 1969); Anna Maria Battista, "Sull' antimachiavellismo Francese del Sec. XVI," *Storia e politica* 1 (1962):413–47; Salvo Mastellone, "Aspetti del'antimachiavellismo in Francia; Gentillet e Languet," *Pensiero politico* 2 (1969):376–515; Leandro Perini, "Gli eretici italiani del 1500 e Machiavelli," *Studi storici* 10 (1969):877–918.

24. Fido, *Machiavelli*, pp. 15–19, uncovers Gentillet's own "Machiavellism." Prezzolini, *Machiavelli*, pp. 194–96, shows how Machiavelli's adversaries, like Gentillet, represented both religious and political-economic aversion. Meinecke, *Machiavellism*, ch. 2, advances this thesis.

25. Antonio D'Andrea, "Machiavelli, Satan, and the Gospel," *Yearbook of Italian Studies* 1 (1971):156–77.

26. See Fido, *Machiavelli*, pp. 18–77, for this period.

27. See Edward Meyer, *Machiavelli and the Elizabethan Drama* (Weimar, 1897); Mario Praz, "The Politic Brain: Machiavelli and the Elizabethans," *The Flaming Heart* (New York: Norton, 1958), pp. 90–145; Felix Raab, *The English Face of Machiavelli* (London, 1964); N. W. Bawcutt, "Some Elizabethan Allusions to Machiavelli," *English Miscellany* 20 (1969):53–74; J. G. A. Pocock, " 'The Onely Politician': Machiavelli, Harrington and Felix Raab," *Historical Studies* 12 (1966):265–96.

28. Raab, *The English Face*, pp. 52–53; N. Orsini, "Elizabethan Manuscript Translations of Machiavelli's *Prince*," *Journal of the Warburg and Courtauld Institutes* 1 (1937–38):166–69, and "Le traduzioni elisabettiane inedite di Machiavelli," in *Studi sul Rinascimento italiano in Inghilterra* (Florence: Sansoni, 1937), pp. 1–19; *Machiavelli's Prince: An Elizabethan Trans-*

*lation,* ed. Hardin Craig (Chapel Hill: University of North Carolina Press, 1944), pp. v–xxxii; Irving Ribner, "The Significance of Gentillet's *Contre-Machiavel,*" *Modern Language Quarterly* 10 (1949):154; John Purves, "First Knowledge of Machiavelli in Scotland," *La rinascita* 1 (1938):139–42; Christopher Morris, "Machiavelli's Reputation in Tudor England," *Pensiero politico* 2 (1969):416–44.

29. Bawcutt, "Some Elizabethan Allusions."

30. D'Andrea, "Machiavelli, Satan, and the Gospel." The Epistle contains a comparison between Catherine de'Medici and Queen Elizabeth.

31. On whether Cromwell recommended *The Prince* to Pole, see P. Van Dyke, *Renascence Portraits* (London: Archibald Constable, 1906), pp. 377–414; T. M. Parker, "Was Thomas Cromwell a Machiavellian?" *Journal of Ecclesiastical History* 1 (1940):63–75. Fido, *Machiavelli,* p. 11, interprets Pole as arguing that Machiavelli wrote *The Prince* to expose the tyrant, to make the people hate him, and cause his downfall. This ambivalent interpretation, found in the early Giunta edition, reinforces the legend of Machiavelli's perfidy with his prince. Modern critics such as Mattingly, "Machiavelli's 'Prince,' " have continued this interpretation.

32. The literature on Machiavelli and the English dramatists is extensive. See Meyer, *Machiavelli and the Elizabethan Drama;* Praz, "Machiavelli and the Elizabethans"; N. W. Bawcutt, "Machiavelli and Marlowe's *The Jew of Malta,*" *Renaissance Drama* 3 (1970):3–49; Irving Ribner, "Marlowe and Machiavelli," *Comparative Literature* 6 (1954):349–51; Antonio D'Andrea, "Studies on Machiavelli and His Reputation in the Sixteenth Century: I, Marlowe's Prologue to *The Jew of Malta,*" *Medieval and Renaissance Studies* 5 (1960):214–48; Piero Rebora, *L'Italia nel dramma inglese (1558–1642)* (Milan: Modernissima, 1925); Daniel C. Boughner, *The Devil's Disciple: Ben Jonson's Debt to Machiavelli* (New York: Philosophical Library, 1978); N. W. Bawcutt, " 'Policy,' Machiavellism, and the Earlier Tudor Drama," *English Literary Renaissance* 4 (Autumn 1974):195–209; Paul A. Jorgensen, "A Formative Shakespeare Legacy: Elizabethan Views of God, Fortune, and War," *PMLA* 90 (March 1975):222–33.

33. Vincent Luciani, "Bacon and Machiavelli," *Italica* 24 (1947):26–41, outlines unrecognized traces in the minor works.

34. James S. Tillman, "Pygmalion's Idolatry and Hercules' Faith: Religious Themes in Bacon's Emblems," *SAMLA Bulletin* 43 (January 1978):67–74, uncovers religious themes in Bacon.

35. More's *Utopia* is mentioned in the Machiavelli-Vettori correspondence. Prezzolini, *Machiavelli,* p. 224; see Harbison, *The Intellectual as Social Reformer* for *The Prince* as a utopian document.

36. Irving Ribner, "Sidney's 'Arcadia' and the Machiavelli Legend," *Italica* 27 (1950):225–33; I. Ribner, "Machiavelli and Sidney: the *Arcadia* of 1590," *Studies in Philology* 47 (1950):152–72.

37. See Nadja Kempner, *Raleghs Staatstheoretische Schriften: die Einführung des Machiavellismus in England* (Leipzig: B. Tauchnitz, 1928); Raab, *The English Face*, pp. 70–73; Praz, "Un machiavellico inglese: Sir W. Raleigh," in *Machiavelli in inghilterra ed altri saggi* (Rome: Tuminelli, 1943).

38. Macauley, *Milton and Machiavelli*.

39. Prezzolini, *Machiavelli*, pp. 257–324; Fido, *Machiavelli*, pp. 34–62; Keith Costain, "The Prince and the Provost," *Studies in Scottish Literature* 6 (1969):20–35; Jan Malarczyk, "Machiavellismo e Antimachiavellismo Nell'Europa Orientale del Cinquecento," *Pensiero politico* 2 (1969):434–44. Germany's serious approach is seen in the work of Christ, Schlegel, Herder, Hegel, Fichte, Ranke, Feuerlein, Goethe, Nietzsche, and others. Machiavellism is seen in Spain, from the early plagiarism of *The Art of War* by Diego de Salazar, in Switzerland, where the first Latin version of *The Prince* appeared in 1560, in Scotland, where novelist John Galt applied Machiavelli in *The Provost*, in Holland, where Testard published a complete French edition of Machiavelli, and in eastern Europe, as shown by Malarczyk.

40. Conor Cruise O'Brien, "What Exhortation," *Irish University Review* 1 (1970):48–61.

41. Giuseppe Prezzolini, "The Kernel of Machiavelli," *National Review*, April 8, 1961, pp. 215–17.

42. Taketsugu Tsurutani, "Machiavelli and the Problem of Political Development," *Review of Politics* 30 (July 1968):316–31.

43. V. Vettori, "Dante and Machiavelli in Today's Technological Civilization," *Italian Quarterly* 52 (1970):23–42; F. Fido, "Machiavelli in His Time and Others," *Italian Quarterly* 52 (1970):3–21.

44. Anthony J. Pansini, *Niccolò Machiavelli and the United States of America* (Greenvale, N.Y., 1969); Prezzolini, *Machiavelli*, pp. 336–47; Eric Cochrane, "Machiavelli in America," *Il pensiero di Machiavelli e la sua fortuna nel mondo*, pp. 133–50.

45. William M. Johnston, "Machiavelli on the Teacher Diplomat," *Journal of General Education* 18 (1967):251–56.

46. Richard Christie and Florence Geis, *Studies in Machiavellism* (New York: Academic Press, 1970); Arthur Bochner and Brenda Bochner, "A Multivariate Investigation of Machiavellianism and Task Structure in Four-Man Groups," *Speech Monographs* 39 (1972):277–85; Antony Jay, *Management and Machiavelli* (New York: Holt, Rinehart, and Winston, 1967);

*Machiavelli's Thoughts on the Management of Man* (Albuquerque: Institute for Economic and Financial Research, 1977).

47. Isaiah Berlin, "The Question of Machiavelli," *New York Review of Books,* November 4, 1971, pp. 20–32.

48. Achille Norsa, *Il principio della forza nel pensiero di Niccolò Machiavelli seguito da un contributo bibliografico* (Milan, 1936).

49. Paul Harris, "Progress in Machiavelli Studies," *Italica* 18 (March 1941):1–11; Eric Cochrane, "Machiavelli: 1940–1960," *Journal of Modern History* 33 (June 1961):113–36; C. H. Clough, "Machiavelli Researches," *Annali-Istituto Universitario Orientale, Sezione Romanza* 9, (1969):21–129; J. Gilbert, "Machiavelli in Modern Historical Scholarship," *Italian Quarterly* 53 (1970):9–26; Dante Della Terza, "The Most Recent Image of Machiavelli: The Contribution of the Linguist and the Literary Historian," *Italian Quarterly* 53 (1970):91–113; S. Santonastaso, *Machiavelli* (Milan: Bocca, 1947).

50. At this writing I have begun compilation of such an annotated bibliography covering the years 1935–80 and to include a section on American scholarship from 1900–35, a short list of major books and articles before 1900, a critical introductory essay, and author, subject, name, and title index.

51. John Morley, *The Works of John Morley,* 15 vols. (London: Macmillan and Co. Ltd., 1921), IV, 117.

# Selected Bibliography

PRIMARY SOURCES

1. Italian Editions

*Arte della guerra e scritti politici minori.* Edited by Sergio Bertelli. Milan: Feltrinelli, 1961.

*Istorie Fiorentine.* Edited by Vittorio Fiorini with an introduction by Delio Cantimori. Florence: Sansoni, 1962.

*Legazioni, commissarie, scritti di governo.* Edited by Fredi Chiapelli. Vol. 1: 1498–1501; Vol. 2: 1501–1503. Bari: Laterza, 1971–73.

*Legazioni e commissarie.* Edited by Sergio Bertelli. 3 vols. Milan: Feltrinelli, 1964.

*Lettere.* Edited by Franco Gaeta. Milan: Feltrinelli, 1961.

*Le opere.* Edited by P. Fanfani, L. Passerini, and G. Milanesi. 6 vols. Florence: Tipografia Cenniniana, 1873–77.

*Il principe di Niccolò Machiavelli.* Edited by Giuseppe Lisio. Florence: Sansoni, 1899.

*Il principe e Discorsi sopra la prima deca di Tito Livio.* Edited by Giuliano Procacci and Sergio Bertelli. Milan: Feltrinelli, 1960.

*Il principe.* Edited by Federico Chabod and Luigi Firpo. 5th edition. Turin: Einaudi, 1966.

*Il principe.* Edited by L. Arthur Burd. Oxford: Clarendon Press, 1891.

*Il teatro e tutti gli scritti letterari.* Edited by Franco Gaeta. Milan: Feltrinelli, 1965.

*Tutte le opere.* Edited by Mario Martelli. Florence: Sansoni, 1971.

*Tutte le opere storiche e letterarie.* Edited by Guido Mazzoni and Mario Casella. Florence: G. Barbera, 1929.


2. English Translations

*The Art of War.* Introduction by Neal Wood. Indianapolis: Bobbs-Merrill, 1965. Revised edition of the unreliable Ellis Farneworth Translation with introduction, drawings, and index.

*The Art of War.* Translated by Peter Whitehorne in 1560. *The Tudor Translations.* Edited by W. E. Henley. Introduction by Henry Crust. Vol. 39. London: David Nutt, 1905; Reprinted, New York: AMS Press, 1967. Earliest English translation of *The Art of War.*

*The Chief Works and Others.* Translated by Allan H. Gilbert. 3 vols. Durham: Duke University Press, 1965. A generally reliable, carefully compiled, but incomplete translation of the major works with a useful index.

*Clizia.* Introduction and translation by Oliver Evans. Great Neck, N.Y.: Barron's, 1962. A good translation.

*The Discourses of Niccolò Machiavelli.* Translated by Leslie J. Walker. 2 vols. New Haven: Yale University Press, 1950. Indispensable scholarly translation with elaborate notes, tables, indexes, and introduction.

*The Florentine History.* Translated by Thomas Bedingfeld in 1595. *The Tudor Translations.* Edited by W. E. Henley. Introduction by Henry Crust. Vol. 40. London: David Nutt, 1905; Reprinted, New York: AMS Press, 1967. Earliest English translation of *The History of Florence.*

*The Historical, Political, and Diplomatic Writings of Niccolò Machiavelli.* Translated by Christian E. Detmold. 4 vols. Boston: Houghton, Mifflin, 1882. Inaccurate translation of the bulk of official writings.

*The History of Florence and Other Selections.* Edited by M. P. Gilmore and translated by Judith A. Rawson. New York: Twayne, 1970. Good translation of major historical works.

*The Letters of Machiavelli: A Selection of His Letters.* Translated and edited by Allan H. Gilbert. New York: Capricorn Books, 1961. Well-translated selection of personal letters.

*The Literary Works of Machiavelli.* Edited and translated by J. R. Hale. London: Oxford University Press, 1961. A competent translation.

*Lust and Liberty: The Poems of Machiavelli.* Translated by Joseph Tusiani. New York: Ivan Obolensky, 1963. A free translation with only adequate introduction and notes.

*Mandragola.* Translated and edited by Anne Paolucci and Henry Paolucci. Indianapolis: Bobbs-Merrill, 1957. A readable translation, although not always successful in capturing linguistic and comic subtleties.

*Mandragola.* Translated by Mera J. Flaumenhaft. Prospect Heights, Ill.: Waveland Press, 1980. A much-needed literal translation superceding less faithful, less accurate versions.

*The Prince and Other Works.* Edited by Allan H. Gilbert. New York: Farrar, Straus, 1941. A good, readable, well-indexed English version of some of Machiavelli's major works.

*The Prince.* Translated and Edited by Robert M. Adams. New York: Norton, 1977. Adequate translation anthologizing criticism useful for the classroom.

*The Prince.* Translated by Edward Dacres in 1640. *The Tudor Translations.* Edited by W. E. Henley. Introduction by Henry Crust. Vol. 39. London: David Nutt, 1905; Reprinted New York: AMS Press, 1967. One of the earliest English translations of *The Prince.*

*The Prince.* Translated, introduced, and annotated by James B. Atkinson. Indianapolis: Bobbs-Merrill, 1976. A scholarly edition with an excellent introduction, ample notes set on the page opposite to the text, information on textual variants and interpretation, and rich index.

## SECONDARY SOURCES

Anglo, Sydney. *Machiavelli: A Dissection.* New York: Harcourt, Brace, 1969. A brave attempt to correct common misconceptions by sketching an informing context.

Barberi Squarotti, Giorgio. *La forma tragica del Principe e altri saggi sul Machiavelli.* Florence: Olschki, 1966. An important, but difficult analysis of structure and style.

Baron, Hans. "Machiavelli: The Republican Citizen and the Author of *The Prince.*" *English Historical Review* 76 (1961):217–53. On Machiavelli's republican and monarchical views.

———. "The *Principe* and the Puzzle of the Date of the *Discorsi.*" *Bibliothèque d'Humanisme et Renaissance* 28 (1956):405–28. One of several significant essays by this scholar on the dating of the *Discourses* and *The Prince.*

Bondanella, Peter. *Machiavelli and the Art of Renaissance History.* Detroit: Wayne State University Press, 1973. A much-needed focus on the rhetorical qualities of Machiavelli's prose.

Cantimori, Delio. "Rhetoric and Politics in Italian Humanism." *Journal of the Warburg and Courtauld Institutes* 1 (1937–38):83–102. Seminal essay on the Florentine humanists, the humanist tradition, and its relevance to Machiavelli.

Chabod, Federico. *Scritti su Machiavelli.* Turin: Einaudi, 1964. One of several perceptive works by this scholar on Machiavelli's thought, method, and style.

Chiappelli, Fredi. *Studi sul linguaggio del Machiavelli.* Florence: Le Monnier, 1952. A meticulous philological study.

De Mattei, Rodolfo. *Dal premachiavellismo all'antimachiavellismo.* Florence: Sansoni, 1969. Surveys influence on subsequent generations.

De Sanctis, Francesco. *The History of Italian Literature.* 2 vols. Translated by Joan Redfern. New York: Basic Books, 1959; Reprint of a 1931 edition. The rambling chapter on Machiavelli contains frequently illuminating insights.

Fido, Franco. *Machiavelli: Storia della critica.* Palermo: Palumbo, 1965. An indispensable history of criticism, particularly valuable for pre-twentieth-century developments.

Gentillet, Innocent. *Anti-Machiavel.* 1576 edition with commentary and notes by C. Edward Rathé. Genève: Librairie Droz, 1968. An excellent authoritative modern edition of Gentillet.

Gilbert, Allan H. *Machiavelli's Prince and Its Forerunners.* Durham, N.C.: Duke University Press, 1938. Studies pre-Machiavelli treatises on the education of a prince.

Gilbert, Felix. "The Composition and Structure of Machiavelli's *Discorsi.*" *Journal of the History of Ideas* 14 (1953):135–56. Argues that allusions in *The Prince* refer not to the *Discourses,* but to a lost manuscript on republics.

———. "Humanist Conception of the Prince and *The Prince* of Machiavelli." *Journal of Modern History* 11 (1939):449–83. Surveys medieval and Renaissance princely literature.

———. *Machiavelli and Guicciardini: Politics and History in Sixteenth-Century Florence.* Princeton, N.J.: Princeton University Press, 1965. Studies interaction of sixteenth-century Florentine historiography and politics.

———. *Niccolò Machiavelli e la vita culturale del suo tempo.* Bologna: Il Mulino, 1969. Studies the cultural context.

Gilmore, Myron, editor. *Studies on Machiavelli.* Florence: Sansoni, 1972. Anthologizes modern views on various Machiavellian topics.

Gray, Hanna H. "Renaissance Humanism: The Pursuit of Eloquence." *Journal of the History of Ideas* 24 (October-December 1963):497–514. Studies didacticism in the humanist concept of eloquence.

Hale, J. R. *Machiavelli and Renaissance Italy.* London: English University Press, 1961. Competent, generalized survey.

Macauley, Thomas B. *Milton and Machiavelli.* New York: Scribner's, 1921; Reprint of a 1868 edition. Landmark reevaluation.

Meinecke, Friedrich. *Machiavellism: The Doctrine of Raison d'État and Its Place in Modern History.* Translated by Douglas Scott. London: Routledge and Kegan Paul, 1957; original German edition, Munich:

R. Oldenbourg, 1924. Analyzes Machiavelli's role in the evolution of *raison d'état.*

Meyer, Edward. *Machiavelli and the Elizabethan Drama.* Weimar: E. Felber, 1897. Pioneer, but outdated study of Machiavelli's influence on Elizabethan drama.

Norsa, Achille. *Il principio della forza nel pensiero politico di Niccolò Machiavelli seguito da un contributo bibliografico.* Milan: Ulrico Hoepli, 1936. An extensive, but unannotated, bibliography of Machiavelli's life and works covering the years 1740–1935.

Pansini, Anthony J. *Niccolò Machiavelli and the United States of America.* Greenvale, N.Y.: Greenvale Press, 1966. An impressive study of Machiavelli's impact in America.

Parel, Anthony, ed. *The Political Calculus.* Toronto: University of Toronto Press, 1972. Contains essays on Machiavelli's thought and methodology.

Pocock, J. G. A. *The Machiavellian Moment: Florentine Political Thought and the Atlantic Republican Tradition.* Princeton, N.J.: Princeton University Press, 1975. Studies Machiavelli's impact on the history of republican political theory.

Prezzolini, Giuseppe. *Machiavelli.* Translated by G. Savini. New York: Farrar, Straus, and Giroux, 1967; original Italian edition, *Machiavelli Anticristo.* Rome: Gherardo Casini, 1954. Still valuable, comprehensive survey.

Raab, Felix. *The English Face of Machiavelli: A Changing Interpretation, 1500–1700.* London: Routledge and Kegan Paul, 1964. An important analysis of Machiavelli's impact in England from the sixteenth through the eighteenth century.

Ridolfi, Roberto. *The Life of Niccolò Machiavelli.* Translated by Cecil Grayson. Chicago: University of Chicago Press, 1963: original Italian edition, Rome: Belardetti, 1954. The most authoritative modern critical biography, scholarly, factual, and well written.

Russo, Luigi. *Machiavelli.* Bari: Laterza, 1974; reprint of 1966 edition. A significant treatment of the major writings.

Sasso, Gennaro. *Niccolò Machiavelli. Storia del suo pensiero politico.* Naples: Istituto Italiano per gli Studi Storici, 1958. A distinguished analysis of the evolution of Machiavelli's political thought.

Strauss, Leo. *Thoughts on Machiavelli.* Seattle: University of Washington Press, 1958. A provocative interpretation of Machiavelli's ironic, rhetorical, and mythical strategies.

Tarlton, Charles D. *Fortune's Circle: A Biographical Interpretation of Niccolò Machiavelli.* Chicago: Quadrangle Books, 1970. A suggestive modern biographical interpretation.

Tommasini, Oreste. *La vita e gli scritti di Niccolò Machiavelli.* 2 vols. Rome: Loescher, 1883–1911. A classic survey now outdated but still deserving scholarly attention.

Villari, Pasquale. *The Life and Times of Niccolò Machiavelli.* 2 vols. Translated by Linda Villari. New York: Haskell House, 1969; original Italian edition, 3 vols., Florence: Le Monnier, 1877–82. Surveys context of life and writings.

Whitfield, J. H. *Machiavelli.* New York: Russell, 1965. Useful, but diffused, study of the major writings.

# Index

(The works of Machiavelli are listed under his name)